12 SIMPLE SOLUTIONS TO SAVE AMERICA

JOHN BURKE

LITTLE CREEK PRESS®

Mineral Point, Wisconsin USA

Little Creek Press®
A Division of Kristin Mitchell Design, Inc.
5341 Sunny Ridge Road
Mineral Point, Wisconsin 53565

Book Design and Project Coordination:
Little Creek Press

Editor: Carl Stratman

First Edition
June 2016

Printed in United States of America

For more information or to order books:
visit **www.littlecreekpress.com**; **www.12simplesolutions.com**
or email John at **jb@12simplesolutions.com**

Library of Congress Control Number: 2016934516

ISBN-10: 1-942586-13-2
ISBN-13: 978-1-942586-13-5

Table of Contents

This book is dedicated to the founding fathers who risked their lives, their families, and their fortunes to create a country that so many of us have benefited from. They deserve better.

❝ I am not an advocate for frequent changes in laws and constitutions, but laws and institutions must go hand in hand with the progress of the human mind. As that becomes more developed, more enlightened, as new discoveries are made, new truths discovered and manners and opinions change, with the change of circumstances, institutions must advance also to keep pace with the times. We might as well require a man to wear still the coat which fitted him when a boy as civilized society to remain ever under the regimen of their barbarous ancestors. **❞**

—Thomas Jefferson

Introduction

When I was in the fifth grade, my mother took me and my two older sisters on a trip to the East Coast. The first stop was the Commonwealth of Virginia. We traveled to Colonial Williamsburg, where I bought a tricorn hat and ran through the maze. From there we went to Jamestown and listened to the story of the first settlers. Next stop: Washington, D.C., where we visited Congress, the Smithsonian, the Capitol, and the White House. I was hooked. It was that trip that sparked my interest in American history and politics, and from that point on, I would play football, basketball, or baseball every day after school and then head home by 5:30 for Walter Cronkite and the *CBS Evening News*.

After graduating from college, I went to work in the family business, Trek Bicycle. My father founded Trek in 1976, and three days after school ended, I started at Trek as a salesman for the Rocky Mountain territory. I had Colorado, Utah, Wyoming, New Mexico, and parts of Texas, Nebraska, and Idaho. It was a big territory, and I drove my Chevrolet Cavalier station wagon 65,000 miles a year visiting customers. I started when Trek was riding high, but times quickly changed. The bicycle retailers did not like Trek, and Trek management did not like the bicycle retailers. I had a front row seat to watch the family business come crashing down. It could not have been a better education.

My father—who had spent most of his time running his original business, Roth Distributing—took day-to-day control of Trek and started to turn things around with a simple program: quality products, at competitive values, delivered on time with a great environment for the customer and the employee. After my year and a half on the road, my father asked me to move back to Wisconsin to head up customer service. I loved it. I had spent 18 months getting my head kicked in with problems, and now I could do something about it. Over the years, my dad and I worked together with a great group of people and grew Trek from a small bicycle company with products sold only in the United States, to one of the leading bicycle companies in the world. We worked hard, we had a lot of fun, and we built a great business.

In 2001, after George W. Bush was elected president, I was asked to be on the President's Council on Physical Fitness and Sports. I served for six years on the Council, the last three as the Chairman. It was during this time that I got a taste of the federal government—the good and the bad. At the same time, I was working to advocate for more bicycle facilities in the United States. I met quite a few representatives and senators and learned about the political process. The process never impressed me.

On my many trips to Washington, I would stay near the White House. Every morning I would get up early and go on one of the greatest runs in the world. First stop: the White House, a simple and elegant building with so much history. From there it was on to the Vietnam War Memorial, where I would stop, walk along the wall, look at all the items left behind by loved ones, and read the names. From the Vietnam War Memorial, I would run up the steps to see President Lincoln and stop to read the Gettysburg Address. Next I'd run to the Korean War Memorial—one of the most underappreciated memorials in D.C. Near the back of the memorial, carved into the black granite, is

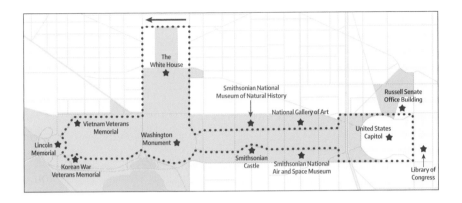

one simple saying: FREEDOM IS NOT FREE. Then I was off to see Mr. Roosevelt, then Mr. Jefferson, then back to the World War II Memorial before finishing at my hotel. I have completed this run at least 30 times, and it *never* gets boring for me.

Over the years, I have become increasingly frustrated with our government. Major problems that require our full attention and co-operation to solve, are mired in partisan politics. The result? Our biggest problems never get solved. The complete lack of progress on major issues, and the inability to make tough decisions, just amaze me. I am a problems-and-solutions guy, and I hate whining. Whenever you bring me a problem, I require that you bring me a solution. I see a great nation in decline, a nation that has done so much for so many of us, and I see politicians on the sidelines do-ing nothing, caring more about their political careers than the state of the nation. To make matters even worse, **over the last year, I have watched as politicians have declared their candida-cy for the presidency with *no* specific plans to solve any of our nation's major problems**. I challenge you to go to the websites of the major candidates and figure out what their plans are for our nation. If elected, what specific action items would the candidates pursue to move our country forward? The people running for the highest office in the land, at a critical point in time, have very few specific ideas about what needs to be done to move our nation forward.

In 2011, my son Richie graduated from Marquette University. I went to the graduation at the Bradley Center in Milwaukee and was looking forward to the commencement address by the author David McCullough. I have read many of his books and was looking forward to the chance to hear him in person. He did not disappoint. The topic of his speech was the importance of reading. "We are what we read more than we realize, and notable readers are most notably leaders." I will always remember those lines. But it was his conclusion that stuck with me, when he gave the graduates some final pieces of advice. McCullough finished with this: "And sometime at some point do something for your country."

On the drive back to Madison, I thought about what McCullough had said. "Do something for your country." What could be my contribution? I love reading and talking about the problems that face the United States, and I have spent the majority of my working life solving problems. I had also recently finished writing a book about my father—a project that I thoroughly enjoyed. I decided on that drive home that my contribution would be to write a short book about solving major problems in the United States with simple solutions.

There is an inspiring plaque by the World War II Memorial. It states the following:

> Here in the presence of Washington and Lincoln, one the eighteenth century father and the other the nineteenth century preserver of our nation, we honor those twentieth century Americans who took up the struggle during the Second World War and made the sacrifices to perpetuate the gift our forefathers entrusted to us: A nation conceived in liberty and justice.

Today our nation faces many complicated issues that present major problems. A national debt over $19 trillion; a 74,608-page tax code that makes no sense; an increase in global temperature of two degrees during the last 50 years that is projected to rise 4 to 11 degrees during the next 100 years; a legal system that is out of control; a Congress that has an average approval rating of 13 percent; and an election process that threatens our democracy, just to name a few.[1] In my opinion, it is time for this generation to *step up* and make some simple, bold changes that will alter the direction of this nation and significantly improve the lives of our citizens over the long-term. It can be done, but it will not happen by accident.

Lincoln observed that the Constitution created a government "of the people, by the people, and for the people." It is time that "We the People" stood up and took responsibility for our government. Our nation has many problems, but each one of these problems has a solution. If we can focus on, and solve, some of our biggest issues, the resulting effect will have many positive ramifications for other problems our nation faces. In this book, I focus on 12 major obstacles we face to move our country forward. I offer simple solutions to all 12. Admittedly, I do not cover every issue that we face as a country. For example, I pass on immigration. Not because I do not think immigration is important; I pass because I do not have a simple solution for it. All of the positions in this book are mine alone. They have nothing to do with Trek. As I have said many times to employees at Trek over the years, Trek is not a political organization. I hope that you agree with some of my ideas, and I hope that you understand that my motivation behind writing this book is to help change the direction of our country. It is not to offend anyone.

I am neither a Republican nor a Democrat. I am an Independent. The ideas in this book come from a perspective of having an open mind and not being tied to one political party. This book takes you through what I believe should serve as America's core values, along with 12 simple solutions to some of the most complex problems America faces. I hope you enjoy the read. ★

Core Beliefs

In my opinion, one of the things we lack in this country is a set of core beliefs. Over the past 30 years, many of our presidential candidates have run on a platform they like to call "American Values." Almost always, the values that candidates talk about are poorly defined, and when they are defined, they typically focus on contentious social issues. All great sports teams, and all great companies, have a core set of values—a list of things that they believe in that guide their organization. I believe that as a country, to reach our potential, we must have a defined core set of values that we use to guide our decision making.

Here are the core beliefs that I think we should rely on to get the United States back on track:

CORE BELIEF #1: Deal with reality.

Great organizations deal with reality. During World War II, Roosevelt and Churchill dealt with reality. They clearly let the people know that there would be tough times ahead, but that in the end we would prevail. Churchill did not mince words. He let the people know that the situation was grim and that they might need to fight the Germans on the beaches and that they might need to fight them in the streets, but that they would prevail. Roosevelt did the same throughout the Great Depression and the war. He clearly let Americans know the dire situation that we faced, and at the same time he let the American people know that if the sacrifices were made that needed to be made, we would prevail in the end.

As a nation, we need to adopt the same philosophy as Churchill and Roosevelt. We need to have supreme confidence that the United States can regain its position as the greatest nation on earth, and that we can be the "shining city upon the hill." But to do that, we need to deal with reality. We need to be brutally honest about the real problems that we face as a country. We need to put all of our major problems on the table and solve them with a sense of urgency. We need public servants who want to talk about serious issues and serious solutions and not be worried about sound bites, raising money, and re-election. We need a group of national leaders who would make the founding fathers proud.

Here are some of the many grim facts and statistics that currently confront our nation:

- We have a national debt of over $19 trillion, roughly equal to $59,000 per person.[1]

- The educational organization ACT recently concluded that 76 percent of high school graduates in the U.S. are not prepared for college.[2]

- The World Economic Forum ranks the United States 48th in math and science.[3]

- Twenty-two percent of children, making up more than 16 million kids, live below the poverty line.[4]

- In 2014, the United States consumed over 19 million barrels of oil per day, which is four times more than the next country in the world.[5]

- The American Society of Civil Engineers has graded America's infrastructure a D+. In the U.S., one-in-nine bridges have been labeled 'structurally deficient.'[6]

- We have a Congress that had failed to pass a budget for 1,448 days. That was almost four years without a budget.[7]

- Our laws are a mess. Two examples include our tax code, which is 74,608 pages long, and the Affordable Care and Patient Protection Act, better known as ObamaCare, which is over 10,000 pages when all the regulations are included.[8] We are a nation run by lawyers creating laws that no one understands. Do you know anyone who really understands our tax code? Anyone who really understands ObamaCare? I know a lot of people, and none of them understand these laws!

Bottom line, our country is massively underperforming based on its true potential.

This country is also a democracy, which means that it's OUR mess.

It cannot be pinned on the politicians in Washington—they will come and they will go. The first step for an alcoholic is to admit that he or she has a problem. The first Core Belief in turning this amazing country around is to get everyone to understand that we are no longer the "Greatest Nation in the World." Rather, we are currently the "Greatest Super Power in the World in a State of Major Decline." It is time to deal with reality.

CORE BELIEF #2: Put everything on the table.

As we look to rebuild this country and ensure that we leave our children with a future that is better than ours, everything needs to be on the table. One of the great mistakes that we make as a country is that we fail to get anything done. We have major problems, and our government does nothing. If the U.S. government were a business, these things would happen:

- The Board of Directors would fire all of the top managers.

- New management would be brought in.

- A new team would be assembled.

- All of the problems would be put up on a white board in someone's office.

- An action plan would be developed for each problem.

- The plan would then be executed.

As poor as the performance has been in the U.S. government, none of the above has happened. We bring in a new president every four years, and then he or she has to run for re-election. The majority of Congress stays in office, and the vast majority of the bureaucracy, no matter how poor their performance, stays in power. We are nearly $19 trillion in debt, it took our Congress almost four years to come up with a budget, we have a tax code that makes no sense, and we still have the same people running the country.

As a nation, we need to put all of our problems on the table and act with a massive sense of urgency. **We need the same sense of urgency that Steve Jobs had when he came back to run Apple in 1997, when he took the company from near bankruptcy to the most valuable company in the world. He put everything on the table, he questioned everything, and he moved fast. We need to do the same.**

CORE BELIEF #3: Shared sacrifice. Everyone needs to contribute.

"Ask not what your country can do for you; ask what you can do for your country." John F. Kennedy uttered these words more than 50 years ago. He asked his fellow citizens to focus on the success of the nation first and themselves second. Yet what does our country look like today? For the most part, we are the "ME" generation. We ask: What can government do for *me*? Tax breaks, new programs, national health insurance—the list goes on and on. As a nation we have gone from being the greatest generation, who focused on what we could do for others, to the ME generation. Even as we face great challenges, our natural reaction has been to ask what the government can do for us instead of what we can do for the government to create a better country for future generations.

The men who founded this nation risked it all. If they had lost the Revolutionary War, they would have been killed as traitors. They fought for a cause greater than themselves. Benjamin Franklin said, "We must all hang together or assuredly we shall all hang separately." None of them were paid, and yet they sacrificed their lives in order to secure a better future for their children. Today, as we tackle some of the greatest problems this nation has ever faced, do we have people who will work for free and for future generations, or do we have people leading this country who put their party or themselves first and put the country second?

As a nation, we lost over 415,000 people in World War II, 36,000 people in Korea, more than 58,000 people in Vietnam, and more than 6,000 people in Iraq and Afghanistan. These are the citizens who have paid the greatest price for our freedom, our democracy, and for our country. Each of us needs to ask what can we do for our country, and then do it.

> As a nation, we need to adopt President Kennedy's words into one simple value: "Ask not what your country can do for you; ask what you can do for your country."

It is also important to understand that no one will ever agree with every decision that is made in this country. Likewise, you will not agree with every decision made at your company, or in your family. It is time to accept that and get over it. It is a lot better to be part of the effort in building something great than to spend your time being bitter and tearing things apart because you disagree with a couple of issues. **The current war between Republicans and Democrats, where we beat the crap out of each other and listen to one-sided talk shows, isn't helping the country.** It is hurting the country. Being open-minded and respecting everyone's position are good and necessary things. In order to move America forward, we need to put the country first and ourselves second.

CORE BELIEF #4: Ensure the U.S. government serves us, the people.

The U.S. Constitution says that the power of government comes from "We the People." Lincoln stated at Gettysburg that the government should be "of the people, by the people, and for the people." If the government was really of the people, by the people, and for the people, then shouldn't the people be really happy with the performance of the government? Shouldn't we strive to have the *best*-performing government in the world? A government with world-class service, world-class productivity, and incredible innovation in the workplace? We actually have that in the military. Think about the Marines. They only recruit the best, they demand high performance, and if they don't get it, they change out the people. This is very similar to the way world-class companies like Apple or General Electric work. They hire the best, demand high performance, and if you don't perform at a high level, you are gone. Our government has a similar attitude when it comes to the military. When it comes to the rest of the government, there is a completely different attitude. Our government is more interested in protecting the status quo and justifying poor performance than it is in putting the best team on the field and making sure that the products and services the government is delivering are the best possible.

In order to turn this country around, we need to start with the government. We should have the best government in the world. In order to do that, the government needs to have the best managers and the best employees. The U.S. government should be a government of the people, by the people, and for the people. We the people should demand a high-performance government.

CORE BELIEF #5:
Apply simplicity to everything we do.

Over time, our government has become too complicated; so many aspects of our bureaucracy could benefit from simplification. Take the following facts, for example:

- The Affordable Care Act and Patient Protection Act of 2010 increased the number of federally mandated categories of illness and injuries for which hospitals may claim reimbursement from 18,000 to 140,000. Did you know that there are nine reimbursement codes related to injuries caused by parrots and three codes of injuries caused by flaming water skis?[9]

- The U.S. tax code is 74,608 pages long.

- There are 14 Department of Education programs devoted to study abroad, 44 job-training programs at a total cost of $30 billion, nine different federal biofuel programs, 159 contracting agencies providing foreign language support, and 76 programs across 15 different agencies to treat/prevent drug abuse. Lastly, there are 679 renewable energy programs in 23 agencies across the federal government.[10]

The United States was founded and governed for more than two centuries on the basis of a document that is six pages long, yet the current income tax code is more than 74,608 pages. We have gone from a simple country to a very complicated country. In my opinion, simple is good, complicated is bad. One of the great champions of simplicity in the 20th century was former Apple CEO Steve Jobs. Jobs believed that less is more and recognized that it takes hard work to make something simple. When Jobs was asked about the success of Apple, he explained, "The way we're running the company, the product design, the advertising, it all comes down to this: Let's make it simple. Really simple."[11]

Here is a recap of the five Core Beliefs that I think our country needs to adopt and apply if we are to turn ourselves around:

1. Deal with reality.
2. Put everything on the table.
3. Shared sacrifice. Everyone needs to contribute.
4. Ensure the U.S. government serves us, the people.
5. Apply simplicity to everything we do.

What follows are my 12 simple solutions to save America. These changes won't solve every problem in America, but if you solve a big problem, there will be a chain reaction that will solve other major issues. A good example of this would be reducing childhood poverty in America. If we can reduce childhood poverty by 50 percent, then many other benefits come out of this change: less crime, fewer people in our prisons, more people paying taxes, and better educated kids, just to name a few. These changes, implemented as soon as possible, would result in massive changes throughout America, put this country back on the path to greatness, and serve as an example to the rest of the world. The roots of our country are democratic: a government of the people, by the people, and for the people. If the people want to change our government, it can be done. ★

Fix Congress

Ask anyone what they think is the most ineffective of our three branches of government, and the likely answer is Congress. Congress has an average approval rating of 13 percent and a deservedly poor reputation.[1] Let's take a look at how bad Congress is and why it needs to be fixed:

1. Congress is in charge of our nation's pocketbook. Not a dime can be spent without the approval of Congress. We have a national debt over $19 trillion which translates to roughly $59,000 for every single American. Congress is responsible for this—not the president.

2. Congress had failed to pass a budget for 1,448 days between 2009–2013.[2] Imagine any business in America, let alone the largest business in America, that does not have a budget. Our Congress is so dysfunctional that we went almost four years without a budget.

3. Money has a major influence in Congress from start to finish. The average Senate campaign in 2012 cost $10.5 million. The most expensive was $42.5 million.[3] In 2008, 93 percent of House members and 94 percent of Senators who outspent their opponents during their campaigns won their respective elections.[4] One of the major problems with Congress is that it is awash with money, yet

Campaign Spending

93%
of House members

94%
of Senators

who outspent their opponents on their campaigns **won their elections in 2008**

Congress has done basically nothing to address campaign finance reform. From 1998 to 2004, 43 percent of retiring Congress members took lobbying jobs after they left Congress.[5] That number is up from 3 percent in 1974.[6] Why are so many Congress members turning into lobbyists? Because corporations are willing to pay ex-Congress members to lobby their friends to influence legislation that might be worth hundreds of millions or billions of dollars. As one example, Congressman Billy Tauzin (R-LA) made almost $20 million as a lobbyist for the pharmaceutical industry between 2006 and 2010. In Tauzin's time in Congress, he helped pass President Bush's prescription drug expansion. As a well-paid lobbyist, his association helped to block a proposal to allow Medicare to negotiate drug prices.[7] That proposal, had it passed, would have saved American taxpayers billions of dollars. The high salaries that lobbying firms are paying former Congress members are actually cheap. Our democracy is for sale, and there is no better example of our government being for sale than Congress.

4. The recent 112th Congress was the most unproductive Congress since the 1940s. In the 112th Congress (2011-2013), 219 bills passed. By comparison the so-called "Do Nothing" Congress (1947-1949) passed 906 bills.[8]

• • •

The following are what I believe to be simple and specific solutions to change Congress from a poorly performing branch of government to a high-performance branch that serves the people and makes decisions in the best interests of the United States.

1. Change the terms and install term limits. We don't need career-long Congress members—that's clearly not working. The 22nd Amendment states that the president can serve two four-year terms. Let's take an idea that is already working and send it down Pennsylvania Avenue to Congress. Put an end to House elections every two years and give each member of the House of Representatives two four-year terms like the presidency. Apply this to the Senate as well. Instead of the six-year terms they currently serve, they should serve four-year terms with a maximum of eight years in office. The House, the Senate, and the presidency would all consistently serve two four-year terms. The benefits of changing the lengths of terms and installing term limits are the following:

- The idea of the "career politician" would cease if the maximum amount of time that anyone could serve in Congress was eight years.

- The amount of campaign money in government would be reduced. Much of the money that flows into campaigns goes to candidates who have been in office for many years and already have power.

Percentage of retiring Congress members who took lobbying jobs after they left Congress

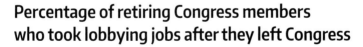

1974	From 1998 to 2004
3%	43%

> **Money flows to power, and the longer you serve, the more power you have. The more power you have, the more money you get. This ends up being a vicious cycle, and it has been demonstrated in our Congress.**

Term limits would serve to take power from career politicians and those who fund their campaigns, and send it back to the people they are serving.

• Members of Congress would begin to focus on solving the nation's problems instead of running for re-election. Today's politicians spend roughly 20 percent of their time raising money for the next election. By putting term limits in place, we would significantly reduce the amount of time politicians spend raising money, allowing our nation's elected officials the ability to spend more time solving the problems of the nation.

• The quality of political candidates would improve. By imposing term limits, we are more likely to attract political candidates who are interested in serving their country, not in creating a career.

2. Change the pay and benefits for members of Congress.
I propose that if a member of Congress has a net worth of more than $2 million, then they should not receive compensation. That is a total of 130 members of Congress and Senators.[9] Such powerful positions should represent what our founding fathers intended—public service rather than a career with excellent pay and benefits. Members of Congress with a net worth of less than $2 million should be entitled to current compensation and expenses. In addition, I believe that the pension program for Congress—which currently kicks in after five years for members 62 or older, and averages more than $40,000 per person—should be terminated.[10] Congress survived without a pension program until 1942, and with our current financial state, we

should not be paying Congress a pension. I don't believe that applying these rules would result in less qualified individuals running for Congress. In fact, I am betting that we will get a better group of people interested in the job. The benefits of not offering compensation to those who don't qualify due to their already high net worth would be the following:

- The message would be clear that the U.S. government is built on public service, and those who rise to the occasion are making a sacrifice and serving their country.

- We would enjoy a tremendous cost savings: This solution would save the United States millions of dollars.

3. Cut the size of the House of Representatives from 435 to 221.

Leave the current states with one Congressman in place and cut every other state's delegation in half. Try and imagine what it would be like to make decisions with 435 people involved in the process. Imagine a school board with 435 members, or how about a company's board of directors with 435 members? Impossible? Why should our government—the government of the people, by the people, and for the people—have a House with 435 members! Is that size of an organization our best chance for success as a country? Not a chance! A simple solution is to cut the size of Congress from 435 down to 221 members. By reducing the size of Congress, the nation would benefit from the following:

- **Better and faster decisions.** With 214 fewer Congress members, the decision-making process would speed up, and the quality of decisions would be better.

- **Relationship building.** In a democracy, building consensus is important. Significantly fewer members of Congress would increase the ability for members from both sides of the aisle to develop more productive relationships.

- **More effective members.** The members of a 221-person House are significantly more powerful than members of a 435-person House. The 221 House seats would be significantly more desirable, and we the people would attract better talent if candidates knew they could really make a difference.

- **Cost**. As a nation we are deeply in debt. By reducing the number of Congress members to 221, this move would not just eliminate 214 members of Congress; this would also eliminate 214 congressional offices. According to *USA Today*, the average congressional office cost $1.45 million in 2011.[11] Total cost savings of eliminating 214 Congressional districts would be $310.3 million a year, or more than $3 billion over a 10-year period!

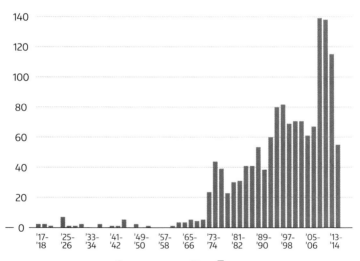

Motion Sickness

Number of motions to end a filibuster in each
two-year session of Congress

Source: US Senate / Mother Jones

4. Eliminate the filibuster. In the Senate today, a group of 41 Senators can filibuster any legislation. This results in the minority being able to carry the day, and this often creates gridlock. Our government needs to focus on getting resolutions through and reducing gridlock. We would increase the performance of our government by eliminating the filibuster.

5. Give the president the line-item veto. Currently 44 state governors have a line-item veto.[12] I find it crazy to hold Congress accountable for all the spending in the United States without someone having the ability to veto certain lines in the budget. It is time that we give this power to the president, whether he or she is a Democrat or a Republican.

6. End gerrymandering. There should be an amendment to the Constitution regarding gerrymandering—the practice of re-drawing congressional districts for the sole purpose of benefiting one political party. Justice John Paul Stevens wrote a book entitled *Six Amendments: How and Why We Should Change the Constitution*. One of the suggestions that Justice Stevens has is to add an amendment that would require "federal judges to apply the same rules in cases challenging political gerrymanders that they have applied to racial gerrymanders."[13] I completely agree with Justice Stevens. Putting an end to gerrymandering will create state governments that are more representative of the electorate, and will send a strong message to career politicians that they cannot rig the game. By putting an end to gerrymandering, less extreme candidates will have a better chance of success, and so will compromise. For examples of how politicians have rigged the game by changing the borders of their districts to increase their odds of re-election, look no further than the histories of Maryland's and Pennsylvania's third districts.[14]

I offer six simple solutions to take the worst-performing branch of our government and make it one of our best. If we are serious about change in this country, there is no better place to start than Congress. ★

The Gerrymandering of Maryland's Third District

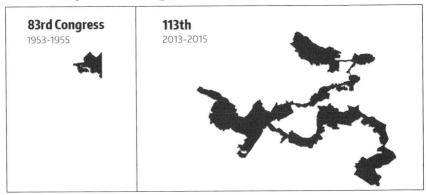

83rd Congress
1953-1955

113th
2013-2015

The Gerrymandering of Pennsylvania's Third District

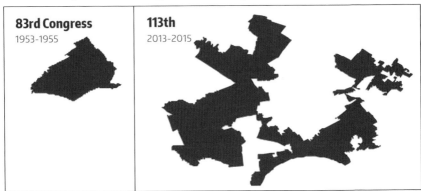

83rd Congress
1953-1955

113th
2013-2015

Reform Campaign Finance

A simple tenet of a true democracy is: one person, one vote. No one's vote should count more than anyone else's. **If the game changes, and someone's vote is worth more than someone else's, then others see the game as being rigged and they will stop playing.** In the end, the democracy that you worked so hard to build falls apart. The situation that we have in the United States currently is that money has infiltrated our political process to the point that the determining factor in who wins a campaign is not who is the most competent candidate or who has the best ideas; it is who has been able to raise the most amount of money. People do not give massive amounts of money to politicians for the good of the country. They give massive amounts of money to politicians to obtain influence. When people give money, they expect a favor in return. This is a horrible way to run a government, let alone the U.S. government.

What evidence exists to support the theory that money in politics is out of control and that the core principle of our democracy is in danger? Consider the following:

- **Elections are won by the highest bidder.** In 2008, more than 90 percent of the candidates who spent more money won their election. In the House, 93 percent of those who outspent their opponent won their election, while in the Senate the number was 94 percent.[1]

- **The cost of elections is out of control.** As reported by Jon Terbush, the average cost of a 2012 U.S. Senate campaign was $10.47 million. Elizabeth Warren spent $42.5 million to win her Senate seat in Massachusetts. The average cost of a House campaign in 2012 was $1.7 million.[2]

- **Congress spends at least 20 percent of its time fundraising.** Would we rather have our public servants representing the people and attending to the nation's business, or raising money?

The average cost of a 2012 campaign

U.S. Senate	House
$10.47 million	**$1.7 million**

The following are two simple solutions to significantly reduce money from influencing our political process:

1. Pass a law to eliminate any campaign contributions to candidates from businesses, unions, or any other organizations, including Political Action Committees. The only contributions allowed should be from people who are actually eligible to vote. We don't let businesses, PACs, or unions vote, so why do we let them donate money? Let's put an end to it.

2. Do not allow out-of-state money in state elections. It is absolutely ridiculous that someone from California can make a donation to a candidate running for governor in Nebraska, and yet it happens all the time. Out-of-state individuals are giving significant amounts of money to candidates in states where they do not reside to influence elections where they do not live. A simple solution is to pass a federal law outlawing out-of-state contributions to in-state elections.

What might be the benefits of these two simple reforms?

1. Presidents, governors, and Congress members would be able to spend significantly more of their time doing their jobs instead of raising money for the next election. Productivity of our highest-ranking public officials would go through the roof.

2. Government officials would not owe favors to big-money contributors. More decisions would be made in the best interests of the United States and less in paying off the big contributors.

3. Better policy would result as government officials would be focused on what is in the best interest of the country instead of what is in the best interests of their next election.

The flood of political donations from sources such as health care companies and defense contractors would evaporate, leaving government officials to make decisions that are in the best interests of the country.

---

4. The current ability of mega-contributors to buy elections would come to an end. Rich donors, corporations, and unions could no longer influence elections with massive contributions, and every citizen's vote would be equal. This would restore people's belief in our democracy.

Lobbyist Fred Wertheimer recently said the following: "We have three elements today: unlimited contributions, corporate money, and secret money. Those were the three elements of Watergate."[3] And as Harvard Professor Lawrence Lessig says, "Today we can do legally everything Nixon had to do illegally."[4]

In the *Federalist Papers #52,* James Madison wrote: "The door of this part of the federal government is open to merit of every description; whether native or adoptive, whether young or old, and without regard for poverty or wealth, or to any particular profession of religious faith."[5] Madison would cringe if he were alive today. The door of the federal government is 100 times more open to politically active people with a lot of money than it is to the average American.

> ## We have a great opportunity to put an end to the days when the few govern the many.

Two simple changes to our laws will restore the democracy that our forefathers built and that so many of our countrymen have died for over the last 240 years. These changes will not be easy; they will be very difficult because those who want to stop reform will pay an enormous amount of money to achieve that. The only way this will change is if the people demand it. These two simple solutions will take money out of politics and force better decision making that will be in the best interests of the American people rather than special interest groups. ★

Create a
High-Performance
Government

The U.S. government—of the people, by the people, and for the people—should be a high-performance government. We the people own our government. Why do we as a nation have a high-performance military yet on the other hand tolerate poor performance in so many other areas of our government? Here are where the problems lie:

1. Public unions do not operate in the best interests of the citizens, but in their own. Public unions make decisions and promote policies in their own best interests. They should because that is their reason for being. They bargain for the best pay, benefits, pensions, and work conditions. Unfortunately, they have used their position of influence to stack the deck against the American people. Even President Franklin D. Roosevelt—one of the greatest presidents that this nation has ever had, who brought the country through the Great Depression and through World War II, the man who was a great friend of the American worker—felt that public unions were a bad idea. "Meticulous attention," President Roosevelt said in 1937, "should be paid to the special relations and obligations of public servants to the public itself and to the government…. The process of collective bargaining, as usually understood, cannot be transplanted into the public service."[1]

2. We have too many "C" and "D" players working in the federal government. We have a lot of great federal government employees who have put in many long hours of public service to make America what it is today. Unfortunately, along with the "A" and "B" players, we have way too many "C" and "D" players on the team. In many government jobs—such as at the Environmental Protection Agency, the Small Business Administration, the Department of Housing and Urban Development, and the Office of Management and Budget, as well as a dozen other federal agencies—your chances of death are higher than those of being fired. According to a *USA Today* article:

> The federal government fired 0.55 percent of its workers in the budget year that ended September 30, 2011. That amounted to 1,668 out of a workforce of 2.1 million. The private sector fires about 3 percent of workers annually for poor performance. That means your chance of being fired in the private sector is six times higher than your chances of being fired working for the government. The 1,800-employee Federal Communications Commission and the 1,200-employee Federal Trade Commission didn't fire a single employee. Last year the federal government fired none of its 3,000 meteorologists, 2,500 health insurance administrators, 1,000 optometrists, 800 historians, or 500 industrial property managers.[2]

Senator John McCain (R-AZ) once said, "The failings in our civil service are encouraged by a system that makes it very difficult to fire someone even for gross misconduct. We must do away with the current system that treats federal employment as a right and makes dismissal a near impossibility."[3]

JOHN BURKE

The American people own the government. The government employees are supposed to work for us. At most high-performance companies, if you do not do your job, you get a warning; and if you continue to fail to do your job, you are fired. Without the ability to fire people, the company has no leverage with the problem employee. Over time, the problem spreads, and a culture of mediocrity sets in. There is no incentive to do an awesome job, and therefore you are left with a poor-performing organization. This is exactly what we have throughout our federal, state, and local governments today. And *you* are the owner of the team!

3. High public wages and benefit programs are causing federal, state, and local governments to cut key programs in order to fund extravagant union labor deals. Public unions' grip on the federal, state, and local governments is forcing cuts in critical programs that benefit the public in order to pay incredibly high benefits to the public unions. "Squeezy" was the cartoon costar in a YouTube video featuring former Illinois Governor Pat Quinn. Quinn put out a video in 2012 to explain that when the state has to pay promised pensions even though there is no money available, other priorities like schools, roads, and law enforcement get squeezed. Unfortunately, after Squeezy's debut, nothing got done.[4] Is this just a problem in Illinois? No, nationwide public pensions are underfunded by more than $4 trillion.[5]

4. Public unions use the political process to rig the game. Under the current rules, the public cannot win with public service unions. Public unions have significant advantages over traditional unions. Through their political activity, unions help elect the very politicians who act as "management" in their contract negotiations.[6] Such power led Victor Gotbaum, the leader of District Council 37 of AFSCME in New York City, to brag in 1975: "We have the ability, in a sense, to elect our own boss."[7]

Over the last 20 years, "public school employee unions have been the single biggest political contributors at the federal level. The $56 million they've spent is roughly equal to the combined contributions of Chevron, ExxonMobil, the NRA, and Lockheed Martin."[8] We cannot have a system in which public service unions spend millions of dollars to influence elections to decide who their management will be and then ask that management to run a world-class organization in the best interests of the American people. Imagine a Congressperson who has received large campaign contributions from a teachers' union making decisions on education policy. Is the Congressperson going to make decisions in the best interests of his or her financial supporters, or make decisions in the best interests of the United States?

Steve Jobs, arguably the smartest businessperson in the last 100 years, and who built the most valuable company on the face of the earth and re-invented five businesses in his lifetime, thought public teachers' unions were terrible:

> But it pains me because we do know how to provide a great education. We really do. We could make sure that every young child in this country got a great education. We fall far short of that.... The problem there of course is the unions. The unions are the worst thing that ever happened to education because it's a meritocracy. It turns into a bureaucracy, which is exactly what has happened. The teachers can't teach and administrators run the place and nobody can be fired. It's terrible.[9]

Elsewhere Jobs said:

> What kind of person could you get to run a small business if you told them that when they came in, they couldn't get rid of people that they thought weren't any good? Not really great ones, because if you're really smart, you go "I can't win." What is wrong with our schools in this nation is that they have become unionized in the worst possible way.... This unionization and lifetime employment of K-12 teachers is off-the-charts crazy.[10]

Businesses need to compete in the marketplace. If someone offers a better product or a better price, the market forces you to react or go out of business. What government unions do is to take competitiveness out of the game. Poorly performing areas of our government can survive because the public service unions protect poor performers. Because poor performers can be protected, progress is difficult to make, creating a less-than-awesome work environment. Great managers do not want to work in the government because it is difficult to make a difference. The government unions win, and the people lose.

• • •

Here are my simple solutions to significantly improve the performance of our government by changing the reign of public employee unions:

1. Abolish public employee unions at the federal, state, and local levels. We have a government of the people, by the people, and for the people. Those who work for the government are already represented by the government and should not be allowed to organize. Franklin Roosevelt was opposed to government unions for good reasons.

2. Implement competitive wages and benefits for government workers based on the private sector and administered by the Department of Labor. We want a government that demands excellent performance and pays our workers well. Take any job and compare it to the private sector, and then set the pay and benefits at the average of what workers in the private sector make. If the current workers like the program, great; if they do not, they should look for another job—just like everyone else in the economy. Give the Department of Labor six months to come up with a simple competitive compensation program. It can be done! A great example is teachers. Great teachers are woefully underpaid for what they do. Pay teachers more, but demand great performance. Can you imagine how many people would want to be teachers if great teachers could make $100,000? Can you imagine the impact that those teachers would have on kids? Can you imagine the people who would want to be principals of schools if they were compensated properly and they could hire and fire the people that they wanted?

3. Review and simplify all pension programs. Have the same board at the Department of Labor review all federal pension programs. These programs should be changed to reflect what is fair to the workers and to the people so that overzealous pension programs are not crippling federal, state, and local governments, and prohibiting these governments from doing what they are supposed to be doing, which is providing services for the people. This means one simple competitive pension program for all public employees in the United States. Give the Department of Labor six months to come up with one simple pension program for all government employees that goes along with the new pay program.

4. Implement a simple review process for all federal employees. This process should follow the following steps: (1) Every public employee gets an annual review; and (2) if a manager wants to remove employees for poor performance, they first get an initial warning. They would then have 30 days to improve their performance, and their manager should specify those issues which must be addressed. Failure to meet the expectations would result in removal from the job. The manager makes the call with approval from his or her supervisor.

• • •

The reasons why the solutions described above would result in a high-performance government include:

1. The performance of every single government organization would significantly improve when everyone understands that in order to keep your job, you need to perform. If you do not perform, you lose

United States Government Performance Review

OPEN TO IDEAS	SCORE 0-5
Has a continuous learning engine; actively seeks new ideas	☐
Is open to ideas from anywhere	☐
Demonstrates a commitment to benchmarking other organizations' best practices	☐
Will listen to feedback and new ideas without becoming defensive	☐
Strengths and opportunities:	

PRODUCTION	SCORE 0-5
Takes initiative to go above and beyond on a consistent basis	☐
Gets things done fast, turning ideas into reality	☐
Keeps commitments and meets deadlines	☐
Demonstrates an ability to execute and implement ideas	☐
Strengths and opportunities:	

ENERGY	SCORE 0-5
Inspires and motivates others with positive energy	☐
Has a high sense of urgency	☐
Leaves drama at the door during conversations and interactions	☐
Promotes a high level of cooperation between their work group and other depts.	☐
Strengths and opportunities:	

DECISION MAKING	SCORE 0-5
Considers multiple sources of information before making important decisions	☐
Demonstrates good judgment and common sense when making decisions	☐
Great at Plan B and adjusting when things change	☐
Deals with reality and makes the tough calls	☐
Strengths and opportunities:	

CUSTOMER SERVICE	SCORE 0-5
Has strong, productive relationships with others in organization	☐
Seeks new and innovative ways to serve customers	☐
Establishes effective, two-way communication with others	☐
Demonstrates the ability to make customers wildly successful	☐
Strengths and opportunities:	

OVERALL AVERAGE	SCORE
Three focus areas to improve:	

your job. In this scenario, the union would not be standing behind you throwing up roadblocks to justify poor performance.

2. The federal government now has a debt that exceeds $19 trillion. By implementing these changes, we would free up financial resources to invest in programs and projects that benefit the future of our country.

3. Public education would improve significantly without public teachers' unions. We should be paying teachers what they are worth, we should let administrators put the best teachers in the classrooms, and all of the attention of teachers and administrators should be focused on education and not political games between teacher unions and the government.

The federal government debt now exceeds
$19 TRILLION

Today we live in a world where over the past 20 years every single product or service has improved, become more affordable, or both. In the private sector, if your product has not improved or become more affordable, you are out of business. It cannot be said that most government services have gotten better and cheaper over the last 20 years. As citizens, we fail to understand that we own the government and the unions do not. We should demand the best government in the world providing the best services at the lowest possible costs. By taking these steps, the citizens of this country can take back the government that was created to serve the people. ★

Fix Social Security

On August 14, 1935, President Roosevelt signed the Social Security Act. What followed over the next eight decades has been one of our nation's most successful and effective programs.[1] Frank Bane, Executive Director of the first Social Security Board, said, "The Social Security Act, our first organized nationwide security program, is designed to meet no less than **five** problems. It is designed to:

1. protect childhood,

2. provide for the handicapped,

3. safeguard the public health,

4. break the impact of unemployment, and

5. establish a systematic defense against the dependency in old age."[2]

The Social Security program, despite all of its critics, has accomplished most of the goals that President Roosevelt set more than 80 years ago.

While most Americans are aware that Social Security provides a retirement benefit, most people do not understand all of the benefits of Social Security:

1. There are 16 million American children who live in poverty.[3] Six million of those children come from homes that receive Social Security benefits.[4]

2. Elderly Americans depend on Social Security. Almost half of the elderly would be poor without Social Security. Currently the program keeps nearly 15 million elderly Americans out of poverty.[5] Only the top 20 percent of seniors, with incomes above $57,960, do not rely on Social Security as their largest source of income.[6]

3. With fewer American workers having pension programs in place, Social Security will be a bigger part of the financial future for people who are retiring.[7]

4. Social Security provides disability, medical, and dependent coverage for employees, their spouses, their parents, and their children. Nearly 90 percent of people aged 21 to 64 who worked in 2014 are insured through Social Security in the case of disability.[8]

• • •

The vast majority of Americans have paid into the Social Security system and are dependent upon its future. Why is a program that has been so successful, and that so many are counting on in the future, on the brink of bankruptcy?

1. The Social Security system is running out of money. In 2024, it is projected that benefit costs will exceed Social Security tax revenues and trust fund income. In 2037, the trust fund will be depleted, and Social Security will then be able to pay only 78 cents on the dollar.[9]

2. Demographics are not our friend when it comes to Social Security. The baby boomer generation is starting to retire, and its effects on Social Security will be massive. According to the *Washington Post* columnist Martha M. Hamilton, by the year 2033, there will be more than 77 million older Americans compared with 46.6 million today. The number of workers to fund the retirees, which today is 2.8 workers per retiree, will fall to 2.1 workers.[10]

3. We have a higher percentage of high-wage earners who do not have to pay any Social Security taxes on earnings in excess of $116,000. When the current cap was put in place, Social Security covered 90 percent of all U.S. earnings. Today Social Security only covers 83 percent of all U.S. earnings.[11]

4. The fertility rate is working against us. Since the 1960s and the advent of the birth control pill, the fertility rate has been in decline. We have fewer young people working to pay for people who are over the age of 65 and entitled to Social Security.[12] This trend is not going away.

• • •

Given the above problems that plague our Social Security system as it is currently administered, how do we fix it? How can we redesign a system that has done so much for so many and remains a program that millions of Americans are depending on to be there in the future? I propose the following solutions:

1. Scrap the cap. If Congress made one simple change and eliminated Social Security's cap on taxable income, $130 billion in additional money would flow into Social Security annually.[13] This amount of money would secure the future of this amazing program, which has done so much for so many. A fair illustration is the following: An assistant to a CEO makes $56,000 a year and pays $3,472 a year in Social Security taxes. The CEO makes $1.2 million or 21.4 times more than the assistant. The CEO pays the 6-percent tax on the first $116,000 of income, or $6,960. The CEO makes 21.4 times more and pays just two times more in Social Security taxes. If everyone paid the same percentage, the CEO would be paying $74,400 in Social Security taxes. Scrapping the cap is supported by 68 percent of Americans,[14] and it would make a huge difference in the viability of the program. This is a major tax increase for the top wage earners in our country. Supporting the Scrap the Cap program is one of the things that the top 1 percent of wage earners in this country can do to sacrifice for the good of the country. In the end, there are millions of people who depend on Social Security, and there is a growing divide between the rich and poor in this nation that cannot stand the test of time.

2. Increase the full retirement age. Americans are living longer, yet Social Security has not kept pace with the increase in average life spans.[15] I propose increasing the retirement age from 67 to 68 as of January 1, 2017, and to age 70 by 2020. This change would save more than $100 billion over a 10-year period of time.

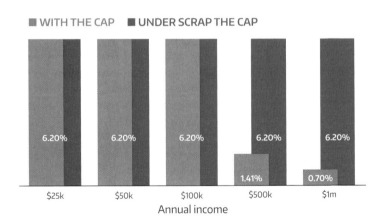

Scrap the Cap

Social Security employee tax as % of income

Source: Social Security Works - Washington | ssworkswa.org

3. Reform the Social Security disability program. The disability program offered through Social Security should be reformed by requiring those who are eligible for disability to reapply for the program every three years. Calls for reform have described this program as a "secret welfare system" with its own "disability industrial complex" ravaged by waste and fraud.[16] Former Senator Tom Coburn, a physician and ranking Republican on the Senate Subcommittee for Investigations, conducted a study and came to the conclusion that 25 percent of people on disability should never have been approved, while another 20 percent were highly questionable.[17] Putting people on disability who should not be on disability is costing our country billions of dollars. In the border area of Kentucky and West Virginia, more

than a quarter of a million people are on disability, which translates into 10 to 15 percent of the population—approximately three times higher than the national average.[18] Even worse is that last year, "the Social Security Administration paid a billion dollars to claimants' lawyers out of its... disability trust fund."[19] Seventy million dollars "went to... the largest disability law firm in the country."[20] You the taxpayer are paying $70 million to one law firm to get people onto disability. A great nation does not let people take advantage of the system. Taxpayers should not be paying for people who do not deserve to be on disability, and we should not be paying outrageous sums to law firms who are encouraging citizens to apply for disability and cheat the system.

Social Security is an amazing program. It provides a retirement program for the vast majority of American seniors, and it provides disability coverage for most American workers and their families. When we talk about the growing income inequality in America, Social Security is one program that provides an income for many of our older workers and a safety net for all American workers. While this great program has helped hundreds of millions since its inception in 1935, it is hanging by a financial thread. All we need to do is show some leadership and make three simple changes, and Social Security will be fixed for the next 100 years. ★

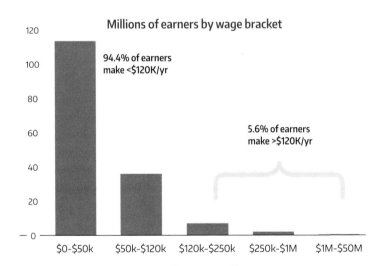

Scrapping the Cap
would only affect 5.6% of Wage Earners

Source: Social Security Administration

Cut Defense Spending

Throughout our history, the American military has kept our nation safe and preserved our liberty and our way of life. Millions have served and many of our fellow countrymen have paid the ultimate price. Our military succeeded in saving Europe in World War I and virtually the entire world in World War II. Our military oversaw the end of the Cold War, and most recently our military personnel have been laying their lives on the line in the Middle East.

Every single American owes a debt of gratitude to the men and women who have served in our armed forces. As with anything, times change, and as a nation we must come to the realization that we currently spend more money on defense than we can afford. This opinion has nothing to do with questioning the men and women who have served in the military; it has everything to do with the recognition that we have a $19 trillion debt and that in order to solve it, we need to put every issue on the table, including how much money we spend in the Department of Defense.

Our national debt has a major impact on our security. Admiral Mike Mullen, the former Chairman of the Joint Chiefs of Staff, has said, "The greatest threat to our national security is our debt."[1] Our current military budget is one of the main reasons why we have such a large debt. To back this up, here are some facts that illustrate just how big of a spending problem we have regarding our military:

1. In 2011, the United States made up 4 percent of the world's population, yet it was responsible for 42 percent of the global military expenditures.[2] We spend more money on defense than the next seven countries combined.[3]

2. The Department of Defense has three different budgets: a baseline budget, plus two "supplemental" budgets. If a particular item misses the first budget, it always has a second and even third chance.[4]

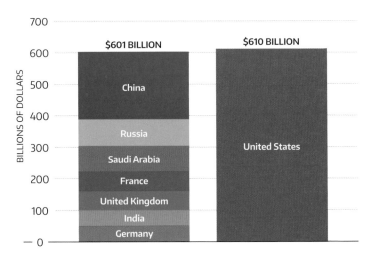

Playing Defense

Defense spending by country
Source: Stockholm International Peace Research Institute,
SIPRI Military Expenditure Database
April 2015. Data are for 2014. Compiled by PGPF
Note: Figures are in U.S. dollars, converted from
local currencies using market exchange rates.

Military Bases

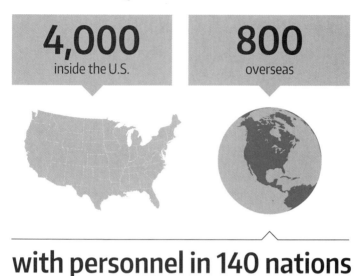

4,000 inside the U.S.

800 overseas

with personnel in 140 nations

3. The American military has many duplicative efforts that result in massive costs. For example, the United States maintains two armies (the Army and Marine Corps) and four air forces (the Air Force, Marine Corps aviation, Naval Air Forces, and the CIA's fleet of aircraft and drones).[5]

4. We have more military bases around the world than we need, but we do not have the political courage to shut them down. The military maintains around 4,000 bases inside the United States and 800 bases overseas with personnel in 140 nations.[6]

5. The United States Defense Department weapons program is massive and not efficient. Currently weapons are designed to be built in key congressional districts; they are not designed to be built in the most efficient manner. One example is the F-22 fighter jet program, which has 1,000 suppliers in more than 44 states. Congress members use their influence to push the Pentagon to appoint suppliers in their district even when those suppliers add to the cost and complexity of the program. Then those same companies who received the work based on politics, make large donations to the same member of Congress to keep the contract. The Pentagon, which is in charge of the Department of Defense budget, cannot do its job of providing the best weapons systems at the most competitive price because Congress is playing politics. The political games that Congress plays with the Department of Defense sourcing is costing the nation billions of dollars. There are a number of members of Congress who, in an effort to benefit their district, want to spend money on military projects the Pentagon does not even want.[7] One example is the production of M-1 tanks. In March 2012, U.S. Army Chief of Staff General Raymond Odierno told the House Appropriations Committee that the Army does not need new tanks, and that the tanks it has do not need to be upgraded until 2017.[8] The Army and Marine Corps currently have 6,000 tanks in inventory. Only 1,000 were used in the Iraqi war.[9] Another example of weapons programs that have grown out of control is the F-35 being built by Lockheed Martin. It is now seven years behind schedule and 70 percent over the initial cost estimate. Senator John McCain called the rise in costs "disgraceful," "outrageous," and a "tragedy." The total cost exceeds $400 billion (the most expensive weapons system in history).[10]

6. The Department of Defense health insurance program is too rich. The Pentagon budgets more than $50 billion per year to provide almost free health care to all military retirees and their families for life, even if they are working in other jobs with health insurance. Former Secretary of Defense Robert Gates tried to reform the Defense Department health care program and failed. In addition, retirement ages in the military were set more than a hundred years ago when the average life expectancy was younger than 60 years.[11] Just like with Social Security, we need to change with the times, and the current health care policy for employees of the Defense Department cannot be sustained. Let's deal with it now.

The good news is that there are hundreds of ways to reduce the defense budget and free up resources that the country desperately needs for other initiatives or to reduce our national debt. Having summarized a number of examples of how defense spending has gotten out of control, I propose two basic ways to cut defense spending. They are as follows:

1. Maintain a single Department of Defense budget. The government should eliminate the practice of balancing three different defense-related budgets and instead maintain a single budget, just like every other company in America.[12]

2. Set a national goal to reduce our defense spending from an estimated \$600 billion per year to \$400 billion per year in 10 years. Military people are awesome at meeting challenges and hitting goals. There are hundreds of opportunities to reduce the budget for the Department of Defense. Let's give the Pentagon a target of reducing spending from \$600 billion to \$400 billion over the next 10 years; then go into the budget line by line and reduce the waste. A few places that we should look at as examples are:[13]

- **Review the Air Force budget and cut the number of planes that we have.** The F-35 and the B-1 planes cost billions to develop and were not deployed in any recent combat zones, including Iraq and Afghanistan. The United States has not been challenged by air for roughly 70 years.

- **Review the Navy's budget and reduce expenditures.** Our current Navy is equal in size to all the navies around the world combined. If we reduced our strategic submarine fleet in half, from 14 to 7 vessels, we could save \$400 billion over the next five years. Another example of excess naval spending is our aircraft carrier capacity. We have 11 naval aircraft carriers, of which the newest generation, the

USS *Gerald R. Ford,* is already billions over the original estimate of $5 billion to develop.[14]

- **Reduce the size of the U.S. Marine Corps.** As a nation we have not conducted an amphibious landing since the Korean War. The Marine Corps currently has more planes, ships, armored vehicles, and personnel in uniform—182,000 Marines—than the entire British Army. That number, according to military experts, could be reduced to 140,000 "with no serious loss of firepower."

- **Reduce the size of the Army.** We could save around $200 billion over the next 10 years by cutting back the Army from around 490,000 to a force of 360,000.

The cost of maintaining the U.S. nuclear arsenal over the next 10 years has been estimated at
$355 billion

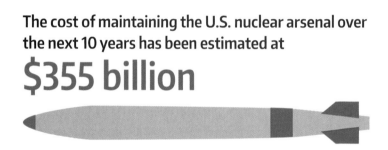

- **Reduce the size of our nuclear arsenal.** The cost of maintaining the U.S. nuclear arsenal over the next 10 years has been estimated at $355 billion.[15] We currently have more than 2,500 nuclear weapons deployed and another 2,500 currently stockpiled. How many nuclear weapons do you want to pay for? The current military plan is to spend $355 billion over the next 10 years to modernize our nuclear capabilities. Do you want to spend $355 billion over the next 10 years when we have so many other needs in our country? Reducing the size of our nuclear arsenal is a great opportunity to significantly reduce our defense budget.

- **Reduce overseas deployment of troops and bases.** We currently have the same amount of troops abroad as we did during the last decade of the Cold War. Reducing troops in Europe and Asia from 130,000 to 100,000 per year would save more than $70 billion over the next 10 years.

- **Reduce Department of Defense health care costs.** Former Secretary of Defense Robert Gates said health care costs for current and retired members of the military were "eating the Defense Department alive." Ten years ago, the cost of military health care was $19 billion. Today that number is higher than $50 billion. Imagine what that number will be in another 10 years? Part of the problem is that military families have not had a premium cost increase in more than 15 years, while other federal workers pay roughly $5,000 or more per year for comparable plans.

- **Change the military retirement system.** The current system allows military personnel to retire after 20 years of service, with inflation-adjusted benefits for the rest of their lives.[16] We cannot afford to have someone join the military at 18, retire at 38, and receive a full pension and health care benefits for life. At the same time, anyone in the military who is wounded in battle and suffers from it should be taken care of. With all of the money that we can

Cost of Military Health Care

10 years ago ⟶ **$19 billion**

Today ⟶ **$50 billion+**

save in the Department of Defense budget, a priority should be to take excellent care of those whose lives have been impacted by the battlefield.

In 1953, President Dwight D. Eisenhower gave one of the most historic of all presidential farewell addresses. What did Eisenhower, a lifelong military man, talk about? The growing military–industrial complex and what he feared could happen in the future. He stated this:

> A vital element in keeping the peace is our military establishment. Our arms must be mighty, ready for instant action, so that no potential aggressor may be tempted to risk his own destruction. Our military organization today bears little relation to that known by any of my predecessors in peacetime, or, indeed, by the fighting men of World War II or Korea.

> Until the latest of our world conflicts, the United States had no armaments industry. American makers of plowshares could, with time and as required, make swords as well. But we can no longer risk emergency improvisation of national defense. We have been compelled to create a permanent armaments industry of vast proportions. Added to this, three and a half million men and women are directly engaged in the defense establishment. We annually spend on military security alone more than the net income of all United States corporations.

> Now this conjunction of immense military establishment and a large arms industry is new in the American experience. The total influence—economic, political, and even spiritual—is felt in every city, every Statehouse, every office of the federal government. We recognize the imperative need for this development. Yet, we must not fail to comprehend its grave implications. Our toil, resources, and livelihood are all involved. So is the very structure of our society.

In the councils of government, we must guard against the acquisition of unwarranted influence, whether sought or unsought, by the military–industrial complex. The potential for the disastrous rise of misplaced power exists and will persist. We must never let the weight of this combination endanger our liberties or democratic processes. We should take nothing for granted. Only an alert and knowledgeable citizenry can compel the proper meshing of the huge industrial and military machinery of defense with our peaceful methods and goals, so that security and liberty may prosper together.[17]

In retrospect, everything that Eisenhower feared has come to fruition. We have a huge military–industrial establishment that spends more than $600 billion a year (more than the next seven nations combined).[18] The military–industrial complex spent $65 million lobbying Congress in 2013 to exert its influence.[19] It is time for citizens to understand what has happened and to take major steps to limit the size and influence of the military–industrial complex. We must start making decisions that are in the best interests of the citizens of the United States, not in the best interests of the military–industrial complex. Just like every business or any individual family, we need to make choices and we need to continuously evaluate our spending. As a nation, we could save over $200 billion per year, which could go towards paying down our debt or to funding other programs that the country desperately needs. If you had a choice, would you spend $200 billion on upgrading our nuclear arms program or $200 billion on upgrading our transportation system? Or $200 billion on cutting childhood poverty in half? Or $200 billion on reducing our debt so that our children don't have to deal with it? We can make these choices. It can be done. ★

Increase the Gas Tax and Save the World at the Same Time

President Eisenhower challenged America to do something great by establishing the Interstate Highway System. Mostly built in the 1950s and 1960s, our transportation system was the envy of the world. It connected Americans from all over the country and drove commerce by making goods available and allowing them to flow freely and efficiently. Unfortunately, what was once the greatest transportation system in the world is today a system in steep decline. Our generation of political leaders has made a decision that it is more important to hold taxes down than to maintain a world-class transportation system. If the United States is to remain competitive in the global economy, we need to change the way we fund our transportation system.

Why should we care about our transportation system?

1. Our nation's infrastructure is rated a D+.[1] This is an embarrassing grade for the largest economy in the world. Our roads, bridges, and railways are in sad shape. You can take a look at the studies and the numbers, and they are all bad. There is no one who says the transportation system in the United States is excellent. More importantly, you can drive around the country and see it everywhere: congestion, potholes, roads in terrible shape. Our transportation is falling apart as our leaders sit on their hands while the majority of the nations that we compete with pass us by. The infrastructures in Europe, China, and Japan are all superior to what we have in the United States.

Our Nation's infrastructure is rated: ⟶ D+

2. Our roads are not as safe as they should be. More than 10,000 motorists die every year due to poor road conditions.[2]

3. Good infrastructure drives the economy. The transportation system does not just matter when you are going from point A to point B in your car. The transportation system drives the economy. The transportation system provides services that support economic growth by increasing the productivity of workers and capital. The better our transportation system, the better our economy will be.

There is a very simple solution to fix the transportation system in the United States. It is called the gas tax. The gas tax has funded transportation projects since 1932.[3] The gas tax at one point in time created the greatest transportation system in the world. For some reason, our leaders decided that it was more important to keep the gas tax down than it was to maintain a world-class transportation system. We got exactly that: a low gas tax and a transportation system in major decline. As we look to improve our transportation system, there is no easier solution than to raise the gas tax. One of the benefits of raising the gas tax is that we would also address one of the biggest issues of our time: climate change.

Why should we care about climate change?

1. The temperature of our planet is heating up. In the last 50 years, average temperatures in the United States have risen by 2°F. By the end of the century, temperatures are estimated to rise another 7–11°F or 4–6.5°F, depending on the amount of greenhouse gas emissions.[4] If that happens, it will be a disaster.

2. The oceans are rising. Scientists have recorded that the global sea level rose about 17 centimeters (6.7 inches) during the last century. The rate in the last decade is nearly double that of the last century.[5] Scientists are estimating that, based on current trends, there could be a 2-foot rise in global sea levels by the end of this century. One-sixth of the U.S. population lives in coastal cities along the East Coast.[6] If what the experts are predicting happens, then there would be serious effects on coastal communities as properties become submerged underwater.

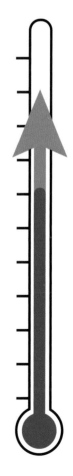

3. The president of the United States thinks it's a big deal. In September 2009, President Barack Obama said that if the international community did not act swiftly to deal with climate change, "we risk consigning future generations to an irreversible catastrophe…. The security and stability of each nation and all peoples—our prosperity, our health, and our safety—are in jeopardy, and the time we have to reverse this tide is running out."[7] And what have we done as a nation? Not much. Whether you support President Obama or not, you should be able to put politics aside and recognize the gigantic threat that climate change is.

4. Americans emit 21 tons of greenhouse gases per capita. This figure is four times the global average, and twice the amount of other First World countries.[8]

5. Ninety-seven percent of climate scientists agree that climate-warming trends over the past century are likely due to human activities.[9]

• • •

How can we take our nation's transportation system, which is rated a D+, and significantly improve it, while addressing climate change at the same time? Introduce a simple solution to kill two birds with one stone. Use the gas tax, which built the Eisenhower Interstate System in the 1950s and 1960s, to rebuild our nation's infrastructure system and significantly decrease the amount of carbon that our nation puts into the atmosphere.

Some people in Washington have proposed raising the gas tax by 15 cents.[10] Let's do something bold and raise the gas tax by $1 per gallon and tax carbon pollution at $60 per ton. This is a *simple* plan that would create the revenue necessary to launch Eisenhower II: a bold plan that would rebuild our crumbling transportation system and encourage American consumers and American industries to be more environmentally friendly, all at the same time.

Percentage of climate scientists who agree that climate-warming trends over the past century **are likely due to human activities.**

The reasons why this plan makes sense are the following:

1. It is simple. Many of the programs dealing with climate change are complicated, such as cap and trade, setting up markets, tax subsidies for wind and solar—the list goes on and on. If we simply put a carbon tax on fossil fuels and let the market do its work, we could get the job done. The country's transportation system is already funded by the gas tax. The simplest solution is to use the same approach. The gas tax is an effective tax. The people who use the roads pay for the roads, and this eliminates many of the complaints associated with other taxes. Ronald Reagan once said, "Good tax policy decrees that, wherever possible, a fee for a service should be assessed against those who directly benefit from that service."[11]

2. It has been proven to be successful in Canada and Sweden. As reported by the David Suzuki Foundation, a gas tax in Sweden, implemented in 1991, reduced the country's greenhouse gas emissions by 20 percent, while Sweden's economy experienced a growth of 100 percent. In Canada, gas taxes are "part of [its] strategy to reduce emissions and encourage investments in energy-efficiency and renewable energy."[12]

3. There are many savvy politicians from both sides of the aisle who also support a plan and have a sense of urgency in dealing with climate change. A great example is George Shultz, former President Reagan's Secretary of State. He became concerned about global warming a few years ago when he saw a video showing the Arctic Sea ice melting. **Shultz drives an electric car and is in favor of taking strong action to address climate change. "The potential results are catastrophic," he said in an interview. "So let's take out an insurance policy."**[13] We have an environmental problem in this world. The less fuel we use, the better off we will be. A higher gas tax would encourage people to buy more fuel-efficient cars and to use mass transportation. This would help the environment, reduce congestion, and have a positive impact on the overall health of Americans.

4. The future trend of transportation is changing. Nearly 45 percent of Americans lack access to mass transit, and a major trend is that young people are driving less and using other modes of transportation more.[14] We need a source of revenue to develop other modes of transportation.

There is an old story about the frog and the boiling pot of water. If you throw the frog into a boiling pot of water, the frog jumps out. But if you put the frog in a pot of water and turn the temperature up one degree every minute, then the frog stays in the water, adapts to his surroundings, does nothing, and dies because he gets boiled to death. This generation has a choice to make. Do we want to be the generation that was presented with unmistakable evidence of climate change and did nothing, or do we want to be part of the greatest generation and make changes with a sense of urgency? By setting a national goal of upgrading our transportation system and reducing the amount of greenhouse gases that we generate, the United States would be taking a global leadership role in both climate change and transportation. These actions would send a strong message to the rest of the world and would set the United States up for success for the next 100 years. ★

Simplify the Tax Code

People don't like to pay taxes—they never have, and they never will. Unfortunately, reducing taxes has become an American sport. We love to reduce taxes without reducing spending. This is how you get elected in America: "I will cut your taxes, and I will cut ridiculous government spending." Reality? Taxes are cut, and no one ever finds the ridiculous spending. Revenue goes down, spending stays the same, and the debt continues to climb. The debt continues to go up so high that we now have a $19 trillion debt that we are going to kick down the road to our kids. It's a great way to get elected, but a lousy way to run a country. While we hate taxes, we have lost sight of the fact that the money we pay in taxes actually provides us with significant benefits. Even though there are so many opportunities for improvements and savings, we do get real value from our tax dollars. Here are a few examples of what your tax dollars support:[1]

1. The running of our government. It's easy to forget that our government has employees and offices, and tax dollars are needed to support this. These are the people we count on to protect our nation, react to natural disasters, to keep our nation healthy by approving or disapproving new drugs, to run and maintain our national parks, to maintain our transportation system, and to educate our children, just to name a few of the responsibilities of our government employees.

2. The existence of public utilities and transportation. The only reason we can drive our cars is because of taxes; it is our government that helps to plan and build our roads and bridges. Critical infrastructures such as the Tennessee Valley Authority and the Hoover Dam were all built by the government. If we were to eliminate government taxes, we'd have to take away all of the roads, the bridges, and the airports. Without taxes, America stops moving.

3. Education. Our public schools and our public universities are other examples of where our tax dollars go. A significant portion of our educational funding comes from the federal government, and without it our public education system would be a shell of what it is today.

4. Public safety. Your taxes pay for the police and for firefighters—basic services that most Americans take for granted.

5. The public safety net. The vast majority of Americans can take care of themselves, yet unfortunately there are millions of Americans who face challenges that they cannot deal with alone. They need help, and the government, through Social Security, Medicaid, and SNAP (formerly food stamps), steps in to help people in need. In reality, our tax dollars are helping people who cannot help themselves.

This is how you get elected in America:

"I will cut your taxes, and I will cut ridiculous government spending."

REALITY? Taxes are cut, and no one ever finds the ridiculous spending.

6. National security. Our national defense, which is paid for with our taxes, has served us well during wartime and peacetime. The national defense has been called upon during the past 100 years for World War I, World War II, Korea, Vietnam, both Iraqi engagements, Afghanistan, the War on Terror, and so much more. More importantly, the investment in our military has sent a message: Don't mess with the United States. Our investment in the military won the Cold War. The only way that the United States is the most powerful nation in the world is because our taxes pay for it. No taxes, no powerful military. Without a powerful U.S. military, we would live in a much different world.

These are just six key things that our tax dollars support. Believe it or not, you get value for your dollar. The way we generate revenue

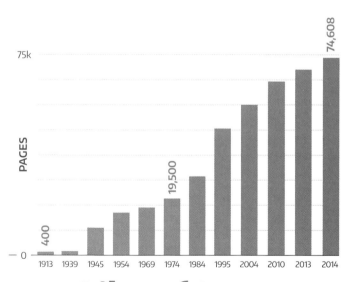

Piles of Pages

Federal tax law keeps piling up as illustrated by pages
in the CCH Standard Federal Tax Reporter

Source: Wolters Kluwer, CCH: 2013; *Washington Examiner*

to keep our nation operating is through our tax system. The one big problem? Our tax system is a complete joke, and it is the best illustration that our nation's government is broken. Congress is responsible for the tax code, and it is perhaps the worst piece of legislation ever created. No one has had the courage to change the tax system because the few who benefit from its complexity have so much more money and power than the average American.

• • •

Here are the reasons why our current system is not working:

1. The current tax code is too complicated. Our tax system is 74,608 pages long, or a total of 12.95 miles. It takes more than 85 pages of instructions just to explain the "short form," 1040A.[2] The current tax code is awesome for tax lawyers but bad for America.[3] **General Electric, one of the largest corporations in America, filed a 57,000-page federal tax return for 2011 and ended up paying zero in taxes on $14 billion in profit.**[4] General Electric has done nothing wrong; they just have the right accountants and lawyers who can figure out how to pay *zero* while making $14 billion.

2. The tax code changes all the time. Since 2001, there have been 4,680 changes for an average of one change per day.[5] How can you keep up with a game whose rules change once a day? Imagine if the NFL changed its rules once a day.

3. The current tax code is expensive, and it eats up resources of both the U.S. government and its people. It is so complicated that a large percentage of Americans pay a professional to do their taxes at a cost of $168 billion a year.[6]

4,680 Changes to the tax code

⌐ SINCE 2001 ⌐

104 Changes to NFL rules

4. There are too many loopholes in the current tax code. For example, Exxon paid $1.1 billion to settle its disastrous oil spill in Alaska. Because of the tax code, they were able to deduct about half the cost. Corporate jets receive faster depreciation rates than commercial airlines because of a tax loophole, and NASCAR is able to depreciate tracks over seven years when the government estimates that tracks really depreciate over 39 years.[7] The list goes on and on. Congressman Paul Ryan made the point that UPS paid a 34-percent effective tax rate while its biggest competitor, DHL, paid a 24-percent tax rate.[8] The tax system makes no strategic sense. It has been cobbled together by politicians who have been influenced by big money over the past 50 years. It is the opposite of good wine. It keeps getting worse with time.

5. Tax breaks are really government expenditures. The reality of the current system is that top earners received an average tax cut of $66,384 in 2011, while the bottom 20 percent saw a tax break of $107.[9] Most people see tax deductions as taxes that they don't have to pay. While that is true, tax breaks can also be considered government spending. There is no difference between $100 that the government spends on a program and $100 that the government gives as a tax break.

· · ·

How do we fix this 74,608-page mess we call our tax code? You start with a clean sheet of paper, and you simplify. Here are my solutions:[10]

1. Simplify the tax code. Set a national goal of reducing the size of the tax code from 74,608 pages to 10 pages. Let's give the American people a tax code that they can understand and a tax code that works for the people, not the special interest groups. This would force out into the open all the deals that lobbyists cut with Congress. If someone wants the government to spend money on a program, then it should go into a budget so that people can see what the program is and how much it costs.

2. Significantly reduce the amount of tax breaks by adopting the Bowles–Simpson Tax Recommendation. Eliminate all tax breaks except the child credit, earned income tax credit, foreign tax credits, employer-sponsored health insurance reduced rates, charitable-giving deduction, retirement savings reduced rates, and mortgage interest reduced rates.

Current Rate	Income Amount	Proposed Rate	Income Amount
10%	Under $9,075	Zero	Under $20,000
15%	Under $36,900	12%	Under $50,000
25%	Under $89,350	20%	Under $250,000
28%	Under $186,350	27%	Over $250,000
33%	Under $405,100		
35%	Under $406,750		
39.6%	Over $406,750		

3. Simplify the tax code by eliminating the Alternative Minimum Tax and personal exemptions.

4. Simplify the current seven-bracket tax system with four proposed brackets.

5. Tax capital gains and dividends at normal tax rates. Both capital gains and dividends are income, just like a salary or an hourly wage. Simplify the tax code, and just call all money earned income. Tax it all the same.

6. Eliminate all corporate tax breaks and reduce the rate from 40 percent to 15 percent. The government should not be in the business of picking winners and losers in the market. Why should oil companies get big tax breaks while running shoe companies do not? Why should certain farmers get big tax subsidies while other farmers get nothing? Our tax system is overly complicated, and we should simplify it by getting out of the business of letting Congress members pick winners and losers with the tax code. If the U.S. government wants to help out a certain industry because it is in the best interests of the people of the United States, then that industry should get a subsidy, and it should be put in a budget so that everyone can see what the subsidy is and how much it is costing the people of the United States, not buried in a 74,608-page document called the tax code.

7. Have the IRS send out a pre-filled tax return, complete with all the relevant information. All you need to do is sign the return and send it back. As described by Cass R. Sunstein, this approach is called the Simple Return and has been proposed by Austan Goolsbee, the former chair of the Council of Economic Advisers. All you would need to do is review the information and sign it. The entire process would take five minutes to complete. This process is already available in California, and countries including Denmark, Sweden, and Portugal are now using it.[11]

By putting this plan in place the following things would happen:

- This plan would generate more than $100 billion[12] in additional revenue and would significantly close our budget gap and start paying off the national debt. We cannot continue to spend significantly more money than we take in. This tax plan would do what Congress has been unable to do: simplify the tax code and significantly increase revenues.

- We would bring some sense of fairness and logic to the tax code. We could take the tax code of 74,608 pages and reduce it to fewer than 10 pages. Americans would actually understand the rules of the game. The simple tax code would also help level the playing field between the rich and the poor.

- This would simplify people's lives. My estimate is that the amount of time to fill out a tax form would be reduced by 98 percent. Look at all the people who are employed in America to deal with taxes. Tax accountants, employees of the IRS, tax attorneys—the list goes on and on. All of those people could be freed up to do something that adds value to the United States and its people.

There is no greater example of how poorly our country is being run than the current tax system. As a nation, we have a great opportunity to say, "Stop the madness! Give us a tax system that is simple and fair and in the best interests of the people of the United States." It can be done. ★

Fix the Legal System

The American legal system is broken. No one comes to America to study our legal system. The only people happy with the legal system are lawyers. Lawyers in America are feasting on a defective system, and because they donate significant sums of money to political candidates, they keep the system intact. In fact, as time goes on, the system gets worse. The worse the system is, the more the legal profession benefits. Anyone can be sued for anything, no matter how ridiculous. The company I work for was sued for patent infringement on a bicycle design. We actually had a real example of the prototype we developed and a mountain of other evidence that we did not infringe. We won the case, but only after spending $3 million in legal fees. Or how about the Trek retailer who held a special event for women? He was sued by a guy for discrimination because the guy was not invited. He settled the case for $17,000 because his lawyer told him that if he fought it, he could lose more than $100,000. These are simply two stories from my experience in a medium-sized business. I have more than a hundred more. There are millions of stories about how our legal system lacks common sense, is overly bureaucratic, and never gets updated or improved. It just gets worse with time.

What evidence exists to prove that our legal system needs a complete overhaul?

1. We have too many lawyers. Our country has too many lawyers, who have produced the most litigious society in history. Former Chief Justice of the United States Warren Burger predicted 35 years ago that America was turning into "a society overrun by hordes of lawyers, hungry as locusts."[1] According to the *Boston Globe*, "With 1.3 million lawyers—more by far than any other country—the United States is choking on litigation, regulation, and disputation.[2] How do we fare compared to other countries? According to *The Economist*, a study of 29 countries conducted in 2006 showed the United States trailing only Greece in the number of per capita lawyers.[3] Even our government is inundated with lawyers: In the 113th Congress, 128 House members and 45 Senate members were lawyers.[4]

2. We have more prisoners than anyone in the world. The numbers don't lie. As reported by Adam Liptak, although less than 5 percent of the world's population lives in the United States, our country's prisoners makes up nearly a quarter of the world's prison population. The United States has 2.3 million people locked behind bars. This equates to 751 people in jail for every 100,000 in population. In comparison, England has 151, Germany has 88, and Japan has 63.[5] Either these countries are doing something right that we are missing, or there are a lot of people roaming their streets who should be locked up. My guess is that we have way too many people behind bars.

3. We are spending a lot of money locking people up. According to the Hamilton Project, a part of the Brookings Institution, the total cost of America's prison system is $80 billion.[6] If the total number of inmates in the United States is approximately 2.3 million, that means the average cost of locking someone up in the United States is approximately $36,363 per year.

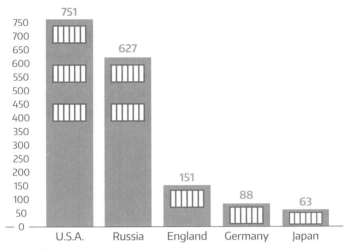

Prisoners per 100,000

• • •

Here are some simple solutions to solve the problems of the American judicial system:

1. Require losers of litigation to pay attorney fees. In the United States, we have a massive amount of lawsuits because people can sue anyone for anything. Why so many lawsuits? Because lawyers encourage people to file lawsuits by not charging them any money unless they win. And if they win, they take a percentage of the winnings. Neither the person filing the lawsuit nor the lawyer taking the case has any real risk. By making one simple change and adopting the English Rule, where the losing party would pay the legal fees *and* the costs of the prevailing party, we would reduce lawsuits in this country by 50 to 75 percent. Lawyers would not want to take on cases that they did not think they could win. The result of adopting the English Rule would be a significant reduction in the amount of court cases in our system, the cases in the system would be dealt with much faster, and most importantly people would not have to suffer through frivolous lawsuits that are costing this country billions of dollars. Companies would not have to deal with goofy lawsuits, and the result would be a significantly better business climate in the United States, which would create hundreds of thousands or millions of new jobs.

2. Set a goal of reducing the American prison population from the current 2.3 million to one million within five years. We have way too many people locked up in prison. Between 1925 and 1975, we had 110 people locked up per 100,000 Americans. Today that number is more than 700.[7] What gets measured gets done, and we should set a goal of reducing our prison population to less than one million within five years. Here are two easy ways to reduce our prison population by 1.3 million and save almost $30 billion a year:

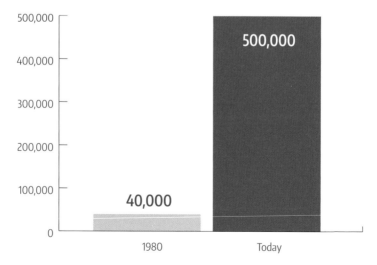

Non-Violent Drug Users in Prison

(1) Reduce the sentences for non-violent crimes, especially drug users. There are almost 500,000 non-violent drug users in our prison system today, compared to 40,000 in 1980.[8] (2) Reduce the prison population by allowing federal and state judges to use their discretion during the sentencing process. Judges are professionals, and they know their business better than legislators. Two Supreme Court Justices have expressed disapproval of mandatory sentences. Former Chief Justice William Rehnquist has said that mandatory sentences are "a good example of the law of unintended consequences." According to Justice Anthony Kennedy, "I think I'm in agreement with most judges in the federal system that mandatory minimums are an imprudent, unwise, and often unjust mechanism for sentencing."[9]

Either Japan, Germany, and the U.K. are right where the average number of citizens per 100,000 people in jail is fewer than 150, or the United States is right where we have more than 700. This is a *huge* difference. There is a great opportunity for us to reduce our massive prison population and save $30 billion that could be put to much better use. ★

9

Fix the Health Care System

Health care is one of the biggest issues of our time. In America, we spend more money than any nation on earth for our health care, and we get horrible results. As reported by *Bloomberg*, we spend $8,895 per person for health care, which amounts to 17.2 percent of our GDP, and this ranks as the highest in the world by far. Yet, for all of the money we spend, our average life expectancy is 78.7 years, which gives us a global health ranking of 46th place. Our friends in Hong Kong spend $1,944 per person and achieve a life expectancy of 83.5 years.[1] What is worse, we are raising the unhealthiest generation of Americans in our history. If we think of the U.S. health care system as an athletic team competing in a league, then we would be the New York Yankees, outspending every other team year in and year out, but, unlike the Yankees, we finish dead last every single year. The worst part about it is that year after year, we tolerate being the highest paid team with the worst results, and we do nothing serious about changing the equation. This would never happen in sports, it would never happen in business, and yet we tolerate this pathetic performance in our nation's health care system.

Despite having the highest costs in the world with the worst results, no one is addressing the real problems of our health care system. As President Obama said, "The greatest threat to America's fiscal health is not Social Security…. It is not the investments that we've made to rescue our economy during this crisis. By a wide margin, the biggest threat to our nation's balance sheet is the skyrocketing cost of health care. It is not even close."[2] And what have we done as a country regarding what the president says is the biggest threat to our nation's balance sheet? Basically nothing.

Gary Player, a golf legend and health fanatic, had this to add about Americans and their health:

> America is maybe the unhealthiest nation in the world because they live on crap. They've got the best food in the world, the best farmers, but they live on crap. When [British chef] Jamie Oliver went to America, he went to areas where children never had cabbage or broccoli or spinach or vegetables in their lives. People are giving their children a soft drink and a doughnut to go to school. No wonder academically they're affected….
>
> Fifty-five percent of the greatest country in the world is obese. How can you compete against the Chinese? You haven't got a chance. People that are lean and mean and working hard and producing maybe 100 engineers to every two or three that you produce. Kids that are learning like crazy at school and spending hours learning. You go to Korea, and those kids finish school at 7 o'clock at night because there's no sense of entitlement. It frustrates me because I happen to have 15 American grandchildren. I love America, but I get so upset at the way I see the obesity. I just don't see how the health care system can work. I pray it does but I just don't see how it can work with this tsunami of obesity.[3]

Gary Player is right: The health of America is a disaster, and our health care system is a joke. How bad is the health care system in America? Here are six key reasons why we should be completely embarrassed as Americans and why we need to do something radical to change the game:

1. Our health care system is out of control. When Medicare became law in 1965, the program was predicted to cost $12 billion in 1990. This estimate proved to be not even close: the true cost of Medicare that year was $110 billion. And since then the cost has escalated, costing nearly $600 billion in 2013.[4] The numbers don't lie: The system is out of control.

In 2010, President Obama passed landmark legislation to transform the health care program in America. What really changed? Not much.

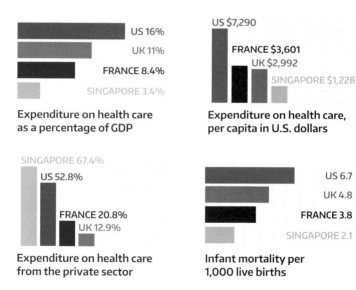

Expenditure on health care
as a percentage of GDP

Expenditure on health care,
per capita in U.S. dollars

Expenditure on health care
from the private sector

Infant mortality per
1,000 live births

World Health
Health care comparisons around the world
Source: OECD, WHO, bbc.co.uk, 14 August 2009

The only major difference is that more people are now covered by insurance. Nothing was done to truly bring down the costs of the program per person and, even worse, nothing has been done to improve the overall health of the American people.

2. The costs of our system today are a disaster; in 10 years, they will be worse. Health care spending has risen from 5 percent of our GDP in 1960 to 17 percent today.[5] The trend is not our friend. Medicare faces significant financial challenges in the coming years. Our population is getting older, and the ratio of workers to enrollees is declining. The total amount of money that our government spends on Medicare, which was $527 billion in 2015, is estimated by the Congressional Budget Office to increase to $866 billion by 2024.[6] The Congressional Budget Office has written that:

> **Future growth in spending per beneficiary for Medicare and Medicaid—the federal government's major health care programs—will be the most important determinant of long-term trends in federal spending. Changing those programs in ways that reduce the growth of costs—which will be difficult, in part because of the complexity of health policy choices—is ultimately the nation's main long-term challenge in setting federal fiscal policy.[7]**

3. A large number of Americans are addicted to the health care system, drugs, and hospitals. In 2006, doctors performed at least 60 million surgical procedures in the United States, or one for every five Americans. No other country in the world gets even close to operating on 20 percent of its citizens per year.[8] It is crazy. As one example, the United States conducts 71 percent more CT scans per capita than Germany does. The cost of those CT scans through Medicare is four times as much as the costs in Germany.[9] If Germany has 100 patients who have a CT scan, the United States has 171. If the cost in Germany is $250, then in the United States it is $1,000, or four times as much.

So a summary of the total costs looks like this:
Germany: 100 x $250 = $25,000
United States: 170 x $1,000 = $170,000

In 2006, doctors performed at least
60 MILLION surgical procedures in the United States, or one for every five Americans.

4. Our health care system is rigged by insurance companies and by politicians who receive campaign contributions from insurance companies. In 2013, journalist Steven Brill wrote an exposé of the exorbitant costs of health care in America. **He reported that since 1998, the pharmaceutical and health care industry "have spent $5.36 billion... on lobbying Washington." For comparison, during the same period the defense industry spent only $1.53 billion.** As Brill summed up: "That's right: the health-care-industrial complex spends three times what the military-industrial complex spends in Washington."[10] The

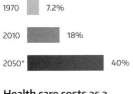

1970 7.2%

2010 18%

2050* 40%

Health care costs as a percentage of U.S. GDP

2010 $2.6 TRILLION

2020* $4.6 TRILLION

Annual U.S. health care spending

1970 $356

2010 $8,402

Average amount spent on health care in the U.S. per person per year

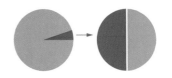

About 5% of the U.S. population is responsible for almost half of all health care spending

Follow the Money

Health care spending in America

Source: Centers for Medicare and Medicaid Services, Kaiser Family Foundation

* projected data

health care lobby has even infiltrated the Senate Finance Committee, which is directly involved with health care legislation and programs. Since 2003, the health care lobby has made campaign contributions to the former chairman of the committee, Max Baucus, of nearly $4 million. The ranking Republican member, Charles Grassley of Iowa, received more than $2 million in campaign contributions from the health care industry.[11] We are going broke, and yet the leadership of this country, the people who make the decisions regarding health care, are taking massive campaign contributions by the people who benefit from the current game. In summary, according to Brill, over $5 billion has been spent by the "medical-industrial complex" to lobby Washington to keep the game the same. The health care industry should be embarrassed. They are responsible for providing this nation with the highest health care costs in the world, along with the worst results, and then they spent $5 billion lobbying Washington to keep the same crooked game in place.

5. Health care pricing is a joke. If you purchase a coffee at Starbucks or a turkey sandwich from Panera Bread, you will pay roughly the same price anywhere you are in the country. Not the same with health care. As Brill reported, Medicare pays $13.94 for a blood test. For the same blood test, Stamford Hospital in Connecticut charges $199.50, and nearby Bridgeport Hospital charges $239. "More than $280 billion will be spent this year on prescription drugs in the United States," wrote Brill. "If we paid what other countries did for the same products, we would save $94 billion a year."[12] Yes, we could cut our deficit or invest in programs to the tune of $94 billion if we paid the same amount as other countries for drugs developed in the United States.

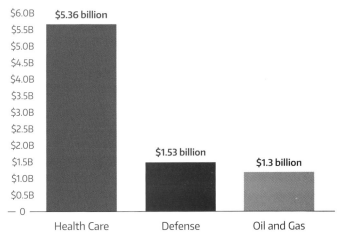

Lobbyist Spending Since 1998

As reported by journalist Steven Brill.

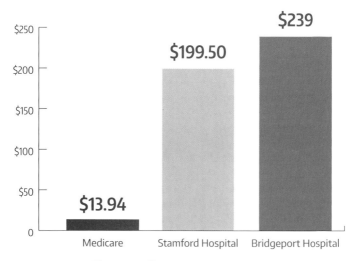

Blood Test Cost

As reported by journalist Steven Brill

It gets worse. Our laws prevent the government from negotiating the best prices for Medicare.[13] Imagine that: The government of the people, by the people, and for the people has laws in place that restrict it from negotiating the best possible price for drugs. The result: Americans pay $186 billion more than citizens in other countries for drugs. How can our government not look out for our people? Our politicians have created a game where the insurance companies and the drug companies win and our citizens lose. For letting the insurance companies and the drug companies play a rigged game, the politicians get massive political donations so that they can run expensive campaigns and keep their jobs. The drug companies keep the politicians in office so that they can keep having off-the-chart profit margins. As a result, we pay far more for health care than anyone else in the world with the worst results, and no one is doing anything about it.

6. The health of the American people is poor. The numbers don't lie. The average American has gained 20 pounds over the last 30 years, we eat poorly, and as a whole we don't exercise enough.[14] We are now the unhealthiest nation in the world. During the great debate about ObamaCare that went on for two years, 99 percent of the conversation was about health care, who gets covered, and who pays the bill. None of the conversation was about improving the overall health of the American people so that we don't have to spend the money on health care in the first place. Why was there close to *zero* attention paid to the root cause of the problem? Because 28 percent of the voters are obese,[15] and if you talk about what it really takes to reduce health care costs—which is unhealthy people taking personal responsibility for their health—you will lose votes. Unfortunately our government leaders are in the business of getting re-elected, not in the business of improving our country and dealing with the real problems that we have.

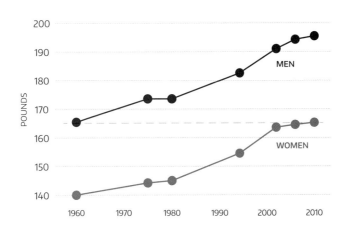

Heavy America
Average weight of American men and women, 1960-2010
Source: CDC | wapo.st/wonkblog

Here are five simple solutions to significantly bring down the cost of health care in the United States:

1. Set a national goal of making the United States a healthy country. If we want to be a great nation, we need to be a healthy nation. We cannot continue to be an obese nation with the highest health care costs in the world. We need to set some basic and unwavering health goals, and we need to energize the nation like JFK did to get this nation to the moon. Let's set the following three goals as a nation:

Three National Health Goals:

1. **Implement the Health Risk Assessment Program for all Americans.** What gets measured gets done, and let's start off by requiring all Americans who receive government-supported health care to take a simple health risk assessment. Once the baseline data are available, a national goal can be set and progress can be measured.

2. **Increase the average life expectancy** of all Americans by two years from 78.6 to 80.6 by 2036.

3. **Reduce the costs of health care** from $8,895 per person today to $6,000 per person by 2020.

Reduce the cost of health care
from $8,895 per person today
to $6,000 per person by 2020

Health Risk Assessment Form

Biometric Category	Low Risk	Points	Moderate Risk	Points	High Risk	Points
Total Cholesterol	< 200	50	200-239	25	≥ 240	0
HDL (women)	> 50	100	40-50	50	≤ 39	0
HDL (men)	> 40	100	35-40	50	≤ 34	0
LDL	≤ 129	50	130-159	25	≥ 160	0
TC/HDL Ratio	≤ 3.54	50	3.55-4.99	25	≥ 5.00	0
Triglycerides	≤ 149	100	150-199	50	≥ 200	0
Glucose	< 100	100	100-126	50	≥ 127	0
Blood Pressure (systolic)	< 130	100	130-139	50	≥ 14	0
Blood Pressure (diastolic)	< 85		85-89		≥ 90	0
Percent Body Fat (women)	< 28%	0	28%-32.9%	0	≥ 33%	0
Percent Body Fat (men)	< 22%	0	22%-27.9%	0	≥ 28%	0
BMI	< 25	50	25-29.9	25	≥ 30	0
Waist Circumference (women)	≤ 35	50	N/A	0	> 35	0
Waist Circumference (men)	≤ 40	50	N/A	0	> 40	0
Tobacco Use	Non-User	350	N/A	0	User	0

	Healthy Male	Unhealthy Male
Height	71"	70"
Weight	186 lbs.	243 lbs.
Blood pressure	103/62	140/96
Percent body fat	20.8%	32.7%
Body mass index	26	34.9
Waist circumference	35	45.5
Total cholesterol	166	231
Triglycerides	86	261
Glucose	85	135
Tobacco use	No	No
HRA POINT TOTAL	**950**	**500**

Source: www.MyInterraHealth.com.

2. Ask Americans to be responsible for their health. We can do this by instituting the following programs:

- Require that any American on Medicare or Medicade take an annual health risk assessment. This is a simple assessment that takes 20 minutes and is a mini-physical. Health risk assessments have been successfully used by companies, and it can help citizens assess the current state of their health. The assessment can also help the government figure out how we are doing as we strive to become a nation of healthy people. If people do not want to participate, that is always a choice, but failure to participate would mean they would forfeit any government health benefits or subsidies. If the government is going to pay for your health care, then you should be able to meet some simple expectations.

- Institute a program where students—from elementary school through high school—take the health risk assessment and then earn a grade for their health that would be included on their transcripts. This would be an effective way to get the attention of millions of students and families. Kids care about their GPAs, and so do parents, and by making their actual health count as a class, it would bring a lot of focus to achieving this goal.

- Put basic nutritional information on every single food item that is for sale, whether it is in a restaurant, a grocery store, or at the ballpark. Americans need to know what they are consuming. Let's make sure that Americans clearly understand what they are eating all the time.

3. Rewrite campaign finance legislation so that the health care–industrial complex cannot prey on the American people. This new legislation would prohibit donations from companies, unions, and political action committees. With this one move, we would prevent the insurance companies, drug companies, and others who make up the health care–industrial complex from creating a rigged game by buying elections with massive campaign contributions. We would free our representatives in Washington to vote for what is in the best interests of the American people, and not for what is in the best interests of the health care–industrial complex.

4. Create "Medicare Lite" to cover all Americans. There has been a debate in this country over the last 20 years regarding government's role in the health of its citizens and participating in the costs. For those who don't like "socialized medicine" or a "single-payer" program, the reality is that we already have one. According to the Centers for Medicare & Medicaid Services, in 2015 more than 55 million people enrolled in Medicare, the nation's health care program for the elderly, and over 71 million enrolled in Medicaid, the nation's health care program for the poor.[16] Put together we now have more than 119 million Americans on a government health program. Older Americans love Medicare. Let's take Medicare and create a basic program called "Medicare Lite" that would cover all Americans. For those interested or in need of a program with more benefits, they would have the option of buying additional coverage from insurance companies. Our friends in Canada have a single-payer system, which yields the following results.[17]

	🇺🇸	🇨🇦
Life expectancy	78.7	81.2
Health-care cost as a % of GDP	17.2%	11%
Health-care cost per person	$8,895	$5,741

This is a system that produces 2.5 years more in life expectancy and costs almost 40 percent less.[18] These are the numbers. Doesn't it make sense that we look at other countries and take their best ideas and put them to work? Companies do this all the time. Sports teams look at other teams and their direct competitors all the time. They do it with an open mind searching for the best answer. It is time that we took our heads out of the sand and looked at other countries for the best practices and put them to work in America. Let's start by looking at health care and look no further than Canada. Just look at the numbers!

What are the benefits of introducing Medicare Lite to cover all taxpayers?

- People who are on Medicare are very happy with the program. Introducing Medicare Lite to cover all taxpayers would result in an even higher level of customer satisfaction.

- Because Medicare is a current program, the infrastructure already exists to manage Medicare Lite.

- The program would allow the government to decide how much it will pay physicians and drug companies.

- This would provide health care coverage for everyone—not just those over 65. For those who say we should not have a government health program, does that mean that we should get rid of Medicare?

- The major reason why Americans spend more on health than any other country in the world is that we spend $450 billion a year on insurance companies.[19] By eliminating insurance companies and buying health care directly, we would recoup billions of dollars.

- This plan would cover basic health care for every American. If you want more than the basic plan, you are free to purchase additional coverage from existing insurance companies.

5. Publish health care results state by state, county by county.
Have the Department of Health and Human Services publish health rankings, including actual health scores from the health risk assessments and cost of health care, once a year, state by state, county by county. Create some local pride in becoming a healthy county. If we have a lot of healthy counties, we will have a lot of healthy states. If we have a lot of healthy states, we will have a healthy country. The rank-

ings would help recognize the best-performing counties around the country, and it would also point out the worst-performing counties so that we could solve the problem. These health rankings would create competitions among communities and would also allow best practices to spread quickly.

There is an amazing opportunity to increase the health of Americans, to increase life expectancy, and to drastically reduce the costs of our health care. As a nation we cannot leave health care to the free market. Citizens now expect that the government pay a portion of their health care, and because of this, the government needs to get into the game and stop sitting on its hands. The government can play a role in significantly reducing the cost of health care and increasing the health of the American people. We don't leave the defense of this nation to private companies and to the market. This is especially urgent when you consider the fact that we currently spend almost 20 percent of our nation's GDP on health care, compared with about half that in most developed countries, and we get the worst results! The time has come to change the equation. Einstein said that the definition of insanity is doing the same thing and expecting different results. We should demand different results, and we should have the intelligence to realize that if we want different results we are going to have to change the way we think about our national health care system.

Trek Health Risk Assessment Program Score

| START OF THE PROGRAM (2008) | **772**/1000 |
| TODAY (2015) | **862**/1000 |

In 2006 at Trek, we had three health-related events within two months. The first involved one of our truck drivers, who had a massive heart attack while driving across Iowa. The driver was a really good guy who was overweight and smoked. The heart attack cost more than $500,000 and put an end to the driver's career. The second event happened to a spouse of one of our employees. His wife, who worked at Trek, decided to get on the company's health program the year before and lost 20 pounds. The husband worked for another company, had poor health habits, and was overweight. He had a stroke, and their family has never been the same. The third event involved a manager in one of our warehouses. He was a great guy—a great big guy. I got a phone call one morning that he had died the night before. He was in his forties and had two young girls. A week later, someone brings me the death certificate. Cause of death? Obesity. I had had enough.

I met with our HR leader and told him that we could do better and I wanted to make some serious changes and increase the health of our employees. Later that week, I held an employee meeting. I showed three slides and told the stories of what had happened over the past two months. I announced that we were going to make two specific changes to our health care plan: (1) we would require that you take a health risk assessment every year; and (2) you had to reach a minimum score. If you did not meet that score, you needed to agree to take proactive steps to improve your health by participating in programs sponsored by the company. Trek offers smoking cessation programs, nutritional counseling, onsite fitness classes, and onsite medical services that include counseling on weight, blood pressure, and cholesterol. Failure to meet the minimum score or to participate in programs intended to address your health concerns would mean that you would pay a significantly higher share of your insurance.

My message was simple. We will give you one year to get on the program, we will provide seminars, individual coaching, smoking cessation assistance, and a fitness center. We will revamp our café to make sure that we have healthy options. But in the end it is up to you.

I will tell you this: I had everyone's complete attention. I figured that there would be some upset employees afterwards, and I was prepared to deal with that. To my surprise, I did not get one email. I did not get one employee visit on the topic.

We care about your health. If you do not care about your health, we are not going to pay for it.

What were the results? Let's take smoking. At the time, the national average of Americans who smoked was 20 percent;[20] at Trek the number was 18 percent. Today that number at Trek is 2.2 percent. When we first started the health risk assessment program at Trek, our average score out of 1,000 was a mediocre 772. Today our average score is 862. We have significantly increased the health of employees at Trek because we were both compassionate and demanding. The biggest winners were the employees. Every year we hold a dinner for those employees who have been at Trek for more than 20 years. The number one comment I get at the dinner is, "Thank you for the health care program. It has changed my life, and my getting healthy has improved the health of my spouse and my kids."

I know that we can turn the health of America around. I have seen what has happened at Trek, and I know the same type of program can work in every company, every school, and many other organizations across the country. I also know that our government, which is paying the bill and setting the rules for health care in this country, could provide a lot better leadership, and if that happened, the results would be amazing. It can be done! ★

Reduce the Risk
of Nuclear War

We have a lot of major problems in the United States: gridlock in Congress, a seemingly insurmountable budget deficit, a broken educational system, and an astronomically expensive health care system. But there is one problem that I believe overshadows all others and which, if we fail to solve it, will destroy humanity. The threat of nuclear war looms larger today than anything else our nation faces, yet it is so daunting that no one really wants to talk about it.

Most Americans don't know these weapons exist in the numbers that they do. Most Americans thought that the threat of nuclear war ended with the Cold War. The raw reality is that the threat of nuclear war is greater today than at any time since the Cuban Missile Crisis. Significantly more countries have nuclear weapons than in 1962, and the information on how to build a bomb is much more available. The Cold War—which in a strange way contained the threat of nuclear war—is now gone. In addition, the sophistication of terrorist groups has changed the nuclear game. Many people have no idea that a single strategic nuclear warhead today is 1,000 times more powerful than the bomb dropped on Hiroshima, Japan at the end of World War II.[1]

We no longer think much about the massive nuclear arsenals that exist in the world. They have been "hidden from public view, thus making it easy for politicians to proclaim 'peace in our time.'"[2]

> **Einstein was once asked how World War III would be fought. His answer: "I do not know how the Third World War will be fought, but I can tell you what they will use in the Fourth—rocks."[3]**

Here is why we should all be concerned by the threat of nuclear war, and why it is the single biggest issue that we face:

1. Because accidents happen. In 1961, a U.S. Air Force B-52 broke up in midair over Goldsboro, North Carolina. It was carrying two Mark 39 hydrogen bombs, and each would have been 260 times more powerful than Hiroshima.[4] Thankfully, they did not detonate. During the Cold War, eight nuclear weapons were lost.[5] During the attempted assassination of President Ronald Reagan in March of 1981, the laminated card, which contains authentication codes to identify the president in case of a nuclear order, was taken from him; it was later found in a plastic hospital bag.[6] We can recover from almost all accidents. Unfortunately, we might not be able to recover from a nuclear accident. It could be the end of the world as we know it.

In 1961 a U.S. Air Force B-52 broke up in midair over Goldsboro, North Carolina. It was carrying two Mark 39 hydrogen bombs, and each would have been **260 times more powerful than Hiroshima.**

2. Because all weapons that are developed end up being used. Hiram Maxim, who invented the machine gun, said, "Only a general who was a barbarian would send his men to certain death against the concentrated power of my new gun." Orville Wright had thoughts similar to Maxim's: "When my brother and I built and flew the first man carrying flying machine, we thought we were introducing in the world an invention that would make further wars practically impossible."[7] Just as with the machine gun, the airplane did not end war; it made war kill even more people. On March 9, 1945, more than 80,000 people were killed and 25 percent of Tokyo was destroyed by bombs dropped from the same planes that Orville Wright thought might make war impractical.[8] There are more than 10,000 nuclear warheads in military service around the world.[9] We are betting that they will not be used. History would say that we are crazy.

A Minuteman III Nuclear weapon travels at a speed of 15,000 miles per hour

3. The amount of time in which a decision can be made regarding the use of nuclear weapons is limited. It is estimated that the president would have 12 minutes to make a decision to launch U.S. nuclear missiles. A Minuteman III Nuclear weapon travels at a speed of 15,000 miles per hour.[10] If you think that a nuclear crisis will never happen, all you need to do is look back at the Cuban Missile Crisis. We were so close to a nuclear war that President Kennedy estimated the odds of nuclear war as being "somewhere between one out of three and even."[11]

4. It is not just the United States and Russia that have the bomb. Who else has nuclear weapons? China, the U.K., France, India, Pakistan, North Korea, and Israel. India and Pakistan combined have approximately 240 nuclear weapons.[12] With the increasing level of global terrorism, we have to worry not only about the 5,000 nuclear weapons that we have on active duty;[13] we need to worry about every nuclear weapon in the world, and that is becoming more difficult to do.

5. Computer systems have problems, and when you are talking about nuclear war, a systems problem could be the end of the world. A computer system failure could trigger a nuclear war. According to Martin Hellman, an expert on issues surrounding nuclear war, "In 1979 and the first half of 1980, there were 3,703 low-level false alerts in the United States alone."[14] Hellman has also written that, "in 1995, Russian air defense mistook a meteorological rock-

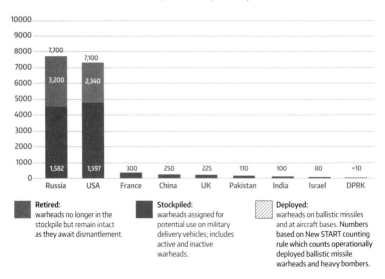

Stockpile of Destruction

2015 estimated global nuclear warhead inventories
Source: Hans M. Kristensen, Robert S. Norris, and U.S. Department of State

Retired:
warheads no longer in the stockpile but remain intact as they await dismantlement.

Stockpiled:
warheads assigned for potential use on military delivery vehicles; includes active and inactive warheads.

Deployed:
warheads on ballistic missiles and at aircraft bases. **Numbers** based on New START counting rule which counts operationally deployed ballistic missile warheads and heavy bombers.

et launched from Norway for a U.S. submarine-launched ballistic missile. Russian President Boris Yeltsin was notified, and a device containing the codes for authorizing a nuclear attack was opened. Fortunately, Yeltsin made the right call and nothing happened."[15]

6. The U.S. nuclear weapons program costs a fortune. As reported by Brookings, the estimated annual cost of the nuclear weapons program in 2013 was $16 billion. Other estimates placed this number at $30 to $35 billion per year. The Congressional Budget Office's projected cost of the U.S. nuclear force for the next 10 years is $355 billion. It is estimated that the cost of modernizing the current U.S. nuclear arsenal could reach $1 trillion over the next 30 years.[16]

7. The greatest nuclear threat today is not the Russians, but the terrorists. President Obama said not too long ago that he's "much more concerned" with the threat of a nuclear weapon exploding in Manhattan than he is with Russia's aggression in Ukraine.[17] In February 2006, Oleg Khinsagov, a Russian national, was arrested on the possession of 79.5 grams of weapons-grade uranium. Khinsagov's intent was to sell the material for $1 million.[18] This is a real story, and this stuff can happen. There is nuclear material all over the world, and the threat of a person who works in a nuclear lab with access to this material selling it to a bad guy is greater than zero. We live in a different world today, and the No. 1 threat of a nuclear explosion is not from the Russians, but from the same extremists who cut the heads off of innocent people; from ISIS, who killed 129 people in the

$355 billion

The Congressional budget's projected cost of the U.S. nuclear force for the next 10 years.

Paris attacks on November 13, 2015; and from Al-Qaeda, who flew the planes into the World Trade Center towers on September 11, 2001.

8. Black swan events do happen. No one thought the space shuttle *Challenger* would blow up, yet it did. Who thought that terrorists would hijack two planes and fly them into the World Trade Center on September 11, 2001? Did anyone think that a copilot would lock his partner out of the cockpit and then crash the plane with 150 people aboard into the side of a mountain? Crazy stuff happens in this world, and the potential for a black swan nuclear event grows with time.

The United States is the most powerful nation in the world. We have used that power over the last century to bring an end to World War I and World War II. We have used that power to bring communism to its knees and end the Cold War. Part of our nation's fabric is that we are leaders. Now is the time to take a leadership role and significantly reduce the threat of nuclear war. In the 2010 documentary *Nuclear Tipping Point*, Henry Kissinger says:

"Once nuclear weapons are used, we will be driven to take global measures to prevent it. So some of us have said... 'If we have to do it afterwards, why don't we do it now?'"[19]

If we were going to act now to avoid a catastrophe that could mean the end of the world, what would we do?

• • •

Here are three simple steps that we could take to dramatically reduce the threat of nuclear war and set a good example for the rest of the world:

1. Significantly reduce the U.S. nuclear arsenal from 5,113 to 311 immediately. Gary Schaub Jr. and James Forsyth Jr., civilian employees of the U.S. Air Force, wrote an op-ed in the *New York Times* on May 23, 2010, in which they recommended reducing to 311 the number of nuclear weapons to be deployed on land, sea, and on airplanes.[20] By reducing our nuclear fleet in this way, we would reduce the chances of a nuclear accident initiated by the United States by 93.91 percent. Imagine getting a phone call telling you to turn on the TV because the president is going to speak to the nation. The president appears on the screen and informs the nation that a computer system problem has caused the launch of a nuclear cruise missile that is heading toward Moscow. That missile will detonate in less than five minutes. He pleads for the Russian government not to respond. How embarrassing would that be?

2. Agree that the United States will not use nuclear weapons as a first-strike option. We should sign the U.N. Resolution 63/36 agreeing that the United States will not use nuclear weapons as a first-strike option and will only use them if someone detonates a nuclear warhead on U.S. land. This agreement would end the possibility of nuclear war being waged over a misguided perceived threat or a misunderstood provocation. If both the United States and Russia agree, the risk of an unintended war decreases to *zero*.[21] In 2008, 134 countries voted for U.N. Resolution 63/36, which would remove nuclear weapons from "high-alert, quick-launch status." Only three nations voted against the measure: the U.S., the U.K., and France.[22] Would you ever want the United States to be the country that started a nuclear war? Would you ever want the United States to be the country that won a nuclear war? Let's join the 134 other nations and reduce the threat of nuclear war by signing U.N. Resolution 63/36.

3. Set the goal of creating a nuclear free world by 2020, and take a leadership role in making it happen. We have done so many awesome things in our 240 years as a nation. Why not lead the world in creating a nuclear weapons–free world? Here is how I envision we could accomplish this goal:

- Lead by example by following through on the first two recommendations. When the world sees that the United States has reduced its nuclear force by almost 95 percent, and that the United States has agreed not to use a first-strike option, we will gain credibility to lead this effort. One expert has calculated that the cost of securing all nuclear weapons and nuclear materials over a four-year time frame would be around $10 billion.[23] We currently spend somewhere between $15 and $30 billion a year on our nuclear weapons program. Let's work with other nations to create a Global Nuclear Free Fund and buy up all the nuclear weapons in the world. What a great investment!

In 1961, President Kennedy spoke before the United Nations, and this is what he said regarding the threat of nuclear weapons:

> Today, every inhabitant of this planet must contemplate the day when this planet may no longer be habitable. Every man, woman, and child lives under a nuclear sword of Damocles, hanging by the slenderest of threads, capable of being cut at any moment by accident or miscalculation or by madness. The weapons of war must be abolished before they abolish us.
>
> Men no longer debate whether armaments are a symptom or a cause of tension. The mere existence of modern weapons—10 million times more powerful than any that the world has ever seen, and only minutes away from any target on earth—is a source of horror, and discord, and distrust. Men no longer maintain that disarmament must await the settlement of all disputes—for

disarmament must be a part of any permanent settlement. And men may no longer pretend that the quest for disarmament is a sign of weakness—for in a spiraling arms race, a nation's security may well be shrinking even as its arms increase.

For 15 years this organization [The United Nations] has sought the reduction and destruction of arms. Now that goal is no longer a dream—it is a practical matter of life or death. The risks inherent in disarmament pale in comparison to the risks inherent in an unlimited arms race.[24]

More than 50 years have passed since President Kennedy spoke of the threat of nuclear war. Unfortunately, we are no closer to "abolishing nuclear weapons before they abolish us." The cold, hard reality is that we are further away. While there may be fewer bombs today, they are more powerful now than at any other time in history. More nations have the bomb, and the potential for new nations and terrorist groups to get the bomb are higher today than at any other point in history. We continue to play a game of nuclear roulette, and at some point in time the gun will go off. This generation of Americans should be the generation that eliminates nuclear weapons from the face of the earth, not the generation that stands by, does nothing, and hopes that we can kick the can on to the next generation. I've offered three solutions to wipe nuclear weapons from the face of the earth. It is the greatest gift our generation could pass on to the next. ★

Reduce Inequality in America

One of the greatest things about the United States is that anyone can succeed. There are countless rags-to-riches stories in America. Every American has the opportunity to rise up the socioeconomic ladder based on their intelligence and hard work. Unfortunately, over the last 30 years, inequality in America has risen, and the ability to move from rags to riches has diminished. Historically, part of the beauty of America has been a strong middle class. Yale economist and Nobel Prize–winner Robert J. Shiller called the rising economic inequality "the most important problem that we are facing now today." Former Federal Reserve Board chairman Alan Greenspan said, "This is not the type of thing which a democratic society—a capitalist democratic society—can really accept without addressing," and President Obama has referred to the widening income gap as the "defining challenge of our time."[1]

What evidence exists that the wealth gap is a serious issue in America?

1. The numbers clearly show that America's famous middle class is shrinking and the wealth gap between rich and poor is growing. In 2011 the Congressional Budget Office reported that between 1979 and 2007, there was a significant difference between the income growth of the rich and the middle class. Whereas the top-earning 1 percent of households had an income increase of about 275 percent, middle-class households had an income increase that was less than 40 percent.[2] There has also been an increase in the amount of pre-tax income that the wealthy 1 percent receive. In 2012, the wealthy received about 23 percent of the pre-tax income. The figure was about 10 percent from 1950 to 1980.[3]

14.7 million children
living in poverty and

6.5 million
who are living below half
of the poverty line

2. Half of the U.S. population lives in poverty or is low-income, according to U.S. Census data.[4] Would you have guessed that? What is worse is that, in this country, there are 14.7 million children who are living in poverty, and 6.5 million who are living below half of the poverty line. The United States in terms of relative child poverty ranks 34th out of the 35 nations in the Organization for Economic Cooperation and Development.[5] How can the richest and most powerful nation in the history of the world finish 34th out of 35 in childhood poverty? How can we as a government plan to spend $1 trillion over the next 30 years modernizing our nuclear weapons program, but we cannot address the issue of childhood poverty? When was the last time you heard a candidate running for the presidency talk about childhood poverty?

Why do we have such a large wealth gap in the United States? And why is it getting larger? This is a complicated issue, but there are three major factors. First, globalization has created a "winner takes all" environment. Companies and individuals who are talented are able to go global. This is great for the few who can play on the global stage, but not so good for those who play on the local stage. Take the iPhone, an amazing global product. Because of globalization, Apple can sell iPhones all over the world and dominate the market. Thirty years ago, there would have been a different company making phones for each individual market. The second major factor is technology. The iPhone has more power and capabilities than the systems that took Apollo 11 to the moon. Computers have increased the quality of life, but they have also wiped out millions of good-paying jobs. Fewer factory workers are needed to build products, fewer accountants are needed to keep track of companies' books, fewer customer service people are needed to help out at the airport, and the list goes on and on. Because of the computer, the world has become more efficient, but there are fewer jobs available. The third major factor that has contributed to inequality is the U.S tax policy. Starting around 1980, the tax code became much more favorable for those at the top of the ladder.

• • •

Why is it so important to address the inequality in America?

1. We are losing a lot of people who do not have hope for a brighter future. Millions of Americans have given up. The lack of a fair chance is costing this country billions of dollars in those who have given up hope. Historically, the growing middle class has provided hope, opportunities, and an incentive for many Americans to climb the ladder.

2. The large inequality gap puts tremendous pressure on the government to take care of people who cannot afford to take care of themselves. The result is increased government spending. Those who are doing well should be fearful of the future. If a large segment of society has no hope for the future, and if that trend continues, then the few at the top will not last. History tells us that eventually the majority of people will revolt. This is what could happen in the United States in the not-so-distant future.

• • •

So, what should we do about this problem? What simple solutions can be found to make sure that the middle class in this country is rebuilt, and that every American has a fair chance at the future? Here are my recommended simple solutions:

1. Increase the minimum wage to $10 per hour—now. The current federal minimum wage of $7.25 just doesn't cut it. This wage adds up to just $15,000 per year. A family cannot pay rent, feed themselves, buy clothing, and buy insurance for $15,000 per year. By raising the minimum wage to $10 per hour, those most in need would receive more money from their jobs. It is far better to receive money from the marketplace in the form of higher compensation than a handout from the government in the form of welfare.

Increase the Minimum Wage
$7.25 ⟶ $10.00

2. Initiate a war on childhood poverty with a goal of reducing childhood poverty by 50 percent by the year 2025. Charles M. Blow wrote an editorial in the *New York Times* in which he made the following point:

> People may disagree about the choices parents make—including premarital sex and out-of-wedlock births. People may disagree about access to methods of family planning—including contraception and abortion. People may disagree about the size and role of government—including the role of safety-net programs.
>
> But surely we can all agree that no child, once born, should suffer through poverty. Surely we can all agree that working to end child poverty—or at least severely reduce it—is a moral obligation of a civilized society.
>
> And yet, 14.7 million children in this country are poor, and 6.5 million of them are extremely poor (living below half the poverty line).[6]

I propose that we pass legislation creating the Every Kid Has a Chance Program with the goal of reducing child poverty by 50 percent in the next 10 years. For those kids who are in poverty, the government would provide a simple program that would allow for the following:

- Three basic meals a day for any child below the poverty line.

- Free basic Medicare for any child below the poverty line until the age of 22.

- Free education for any child below the poverty line, including college education for any child who graduates from high school and is accepted at a four-year college or technical institute.

This program would have the goal of reducing childhood poverty by 50 percent in the next 10 years and, most importantly, the Every Kid Has a Chance Program would create productive tax-paying citizens for the future. Imagine the cost difference over the long-term for a kid born in poverty who stays in poverty, ends up in jail, goes through the legal system, and ends up on welfare compared to the kid who is born into poverty through no fault of his or her own, and is guaranteed three basic meals a day, health care, and a free education. Over the long haul, which program makes more sense for our country in terms of dealing with childhood poverty? Our current plan? Or the Every Kid Has a Chance Program? Which program holds the higher moral ground? Which program costs less over the long-term? This is an opportunity for government to help people who cannot help themselves and save money in the long run by producing more productive tax-paying citizens for the future.

3. Scrap the cap on Social Security taxes. The current program mandates that you pay a percentage of your income into Social Security up to a certain amount. In 2016, that percentage is 6 and the amount is $116,000. So, for example, someone who makes $80,000 a year pays $4,800 in Social Security taxes. Yet someone who makes $10 million or 172 times that amount only has to pay approximately $7,000. By scrapping the Social Security cap, the person with $10 million in earnings would pay $600,000; this would help reduce the gap between the rich and the poor. Another result of scrapping the cap is that the increased tax goes to Social Security, which would fund the Every Kid Has a Chance Program.

By increasing the minimum wage to $10 an hour, scrapping the cap on Social Security, and launching a war on childhood poverty, we would give hope to an entire generation of Americans who live at the bottom of the ladder. These three simple solutions would restore the American dream for millions and would make an investment in the lives of children who, by no fault of their own, were born into poverty with very little chance of making it out. As a nation, we have the ability to increase the fairness in our society and enhance the American Dream for generations to come. ★

Reduce Gun Deaths in America

We have a problem with guns in America. We are a nation with a gun violence rate that is 25 times the average of other civilized nations. The difference is that we lack the simple gun control laws that have made the chances of being shot in the United States 25 times higher than anywhere else in the world.[1] We have debated this issue for the last 50 years with no progress. It is time for some simple solutions to a complicated issue.

Why do we need gun control?

1. More than 12,000 people are killed by firearms each year in the United States (more than 32,000 if you include suicides). Another 75,962 are maimed by gunfire.[2] The number of people who die each year from gun violence in our country is four times the number of people who died at Pearl Harbor (2,403) or lost their lives on 9/11 (2,997). To make matters worse, this happens every single year in our country. Over a 10-year period of time, there have been more than 100,000 dead and more than 750,000 maimed because of gun violence in America. As a nation we should be appalled and embarrassed by these numbers. The numbers don't lie. We have 29.7

murders per 100,000 citizens per year in the United States. Our friends in Canada have 0.51, in Germany that figure is 0.19, and in Australia 0.14.[3] Why is Australia so low? I will give you two guesses: (A) they have the same gun laws as the United States, but they have really nice people; or (B) they had a big gun problem in Australia, and the government changed the laws in 1996 to ban all automatic and semiautomatic weapons.[4] If you picked B, you are the winner! The sad truth is that the United States is the most violent country in the world, and we have done nothing to solve the problem.

Gun Violence in America
10-year period of time

100,000-plus dead	750,000-plus maimed

2. Gun violence is costing the U.S. economy more than $229 billion.[5] Gun violence is so bad in our country that many people overlook the cost. Just think about the health care costs of taking care of the 75,962 people who are shot every year and don't die: productivity lost from those who cannot work, jail costs for those who ruin their lives by using firearms, police costs, etc. Just ask any mayor of Big City USA what would happen to their police budget if the gun control laws in this country were the same as any other civilized country in the world. Answer… significantly less than what they currently are.

3. It is time. Just take a look at presidential history and the gun: several presidential candidates and presidents have been victims of gunfire. In the last 100 years alone, Theodore Roosevelt was shot during the 1912 election; Franklin Roosevelt was shot at after he won the presidency in Miami in 1933; an assassination attempt was made on Harry Truman in 1950, resulting in the death of a White House

294 mass shootings
(when four or more people are shot)
in the first 274 days of 2015
Source: Washington Post

policeman; John F. Kennedy was assassinated in 1963, and his brother Bobby was shot and killed in the 1968 campaign; George Wallace was shot and ended up in a wheelchair in the 1972 campaign; Gerald Ford survived two assassination attempts in 1975; and Ronald Reagan was shot only three months into his presidency in 1981. We have witnessed massacres at Columbine High School in Colorado, where 14 kids and a teacher were killed; at Sandy Hook Elementary School, which resulted in the deaths of 20 children; and many other school shootings have led to the loss of life of innocent school kids.[6] We have seen Congresswoman Gabby Giffords shot in the head and suffer permanent disability, and most recently we have seen a year of gun violence in America that is hard to believe. According to the *Washington Post*, there were 294 mass shootings, defined as when four or more people are shot, in the first 274 days of 2015.[7] Nine people were shot dead in a church in Charleston, South Carolina, and most recently 14 people were killed and 22 injured in another mass shooting in San Bernardino, California. What have we done as a nation to fix this problem? Nothing. Great nations deal with reality, and the reality of the situation is that we need to do something. Ezra Klein, writing for the *Washington Post,* put it best:

> If roads were collapsing all across the United States, killing dozens of drivers, we would surely see that as a moment to talk about what we could do to keep the roads from collapsing. If terrorists were

detonating bombs in port after port, you can be sure Congress would be working to upgrade the nation's security measures. If a plague was ripping through communities, public-health officials would be working feverishly to contain it.

Only with gun violence do we respond to repeated tragedies by saying that mourning is acceptable but discussing how to prevent more tragedies is not.... Talking about how to stop mass shootings in the aftermath of a string of mass shootings isn't "too soon." It's much too late.[8]

4. The world has changed since the Second Amendment of the Constitution was ratified in 1791. The Second Amendment of the Constitution does not guarantee the right of citizens to walk around our streets with assault rifles. **What the Second Amendment states is the following: "A well-regulated Militia, being necessary to the security of a Free State, the right of the people to keep and bear Arms, shall not be infringed."** Do we really think our founding fathers would support semiautomatic rifles that disperse 20 bullets in as many seconds? Clearly not. Their intent was the protection of the nation at a time when there were relatively few people in the military and the citizens had to be prepared. Think Paul Revere riding his horse to warn the citizens that "The British are coming!" At that point in time, our government needed our citizens to be armed in order to protect the country. Today we have the Army, the Air Force, the Navy, and the Marines. In addition, we have police in every city across our country. We do not need citizens to be armed with semiautomatic weapons to protect our country.

5. The majority of Americans support common-sense measures to prevent gun violence. A recent poll showed that 92 percent of Americans support a measure requiring background checks.[9] Yet the gun lobby protects the views of the 8 percent who disagree. Is our government elected to represent the 92 percent majority or the 8 percent minority?

· · ·

Here are my simple solutions to significantly reduce gun deaths in the United States:

1. Rewrite the Second Amendment to the Constitution of the United States. After his retirement, Chief Justice Burger said that the Second Amendment "has been the subject of one of the greatest pieces of fraud, I repeat the word 'fraud,' on the American public by special interest groups that I have ever seen in my lifetime."[10] Justice John Paul Stevens has suggested that the Second Amendment should be changed by adding five words. It should read: "A well-regulated Militia, being necessary to the security of a Free State, the right of the people to keep and bear Arms *when serving in the Militia* shall not be infringed."[11]

2. Ban all assault rifles and extended clips. The gun that was used in Congresswoman Gabby Giffords's shooting emptied 33 rounds in less than 30 seconds.[12] In addition to banning all assault rifles, the government should launch a program to buy back all of these weapons. Pay people what they paid for the weapon, but get them off the streets. In 1996, when Australia banned assault rifles and extended clips, the homicide rate plummeted 59 percent over the next decade.[13]

The gun that was used in
Congresswoman Gabby Giffords's shooting

emptied 33 rounds
in less than 30 seconds

3. Impose a universal background check on 100 percent of guns purchased. A large number of Americans think that federal laws require a background check for every gun purchase and that the law bans high-capacity magazines. Incorrect! More than 40 percent of purchased guns require no background check.[14] In polls, 87 percent of voters and 90 percent of gun owners say they support background checks for all gun sales.[15] Let's give the people what they want and require that all gun owners have a background check. The system is already in place, and this would be a simple solution.

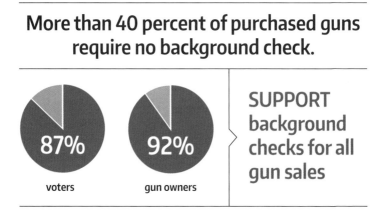

More than 40 percent of purchased guns require no background check.

87% voters

92% gun owners

SUPPORT background checks for all gun sales

4. Require mandatory gun licenses for gun owners. Guns should be treated the same as cars. Why do you need to get a license in order to drive and get a car registered? Because driving a car is a big responsibility, and if you misuse the car, you can cause serious damage, not only to yourself but to others. A gun is more dangerous than an automobile, and people should have to get a license to have a gun. It is in everyone's interest to make sure that everyone who has a gun is capable of safe gun ownership. Right now, you can go to a gun show and buy a gun and never have to get it registered. That would be like having to get a registration for a new car but not for a used one. The NRA has brainwashed people into thinking that it is a bad thing to require that guns be registered. It is not a bad thing; it is a common-sense practice that would benefit all Americans whether you own a gun or not.

More than 12,000 of our fellow citizens are killed every year by gun violence. Another 75,962 are wounded by guns. We are the most violent country in the world. With a few simple solutions, we can regulate guns the same way we regulate cars. We can save the nation billions of dollars and, most importantly, we can save tens of thousands of lives, and prevent misery for so many families affected by gun violence across America. ★

Conclusion

Tom Brokaw wrote a book called *The Greatest Generation*. In his book, Brokaw wrote that the generation who grew up in the United States during the Great Depression, and then went on to fight in World War II and to support the home effort, was the Greatest Generation. He argued that these men and women fought not for fame and recognition, but because it was the right thing to do.

The current generation of Americans, of which I am one, does not have so much to be proud of. The bad news is that we are not leaving our nation in better shape for the next generation. The good news is that there is an amazing opportunity in these difficult times for our generation to step up and solve these major issues. We have the chance to make a difference so that the next generation of Americans is left with a country in better shape than the one that we inherited. Just think about what we could accomplish as a country in the next four years:

1. We could be the generation to reorganize our government and make significant changes to the way Congress operates and fix the gridlock in Washington. We could have citizen legislators instead of professional politicians running our government. We could orchestrate the most significant structural changes in our government since the founding fathers.

2. We could be the generation to reform campaign finance. Ninety-three percent of political candidates who raise the most amount of money win. We allow individuals of great wealth to give candidates unlimited money in order to buy elections. In the United States, elections should not be for sale. We should not be putting elected officials into office based on who is the best fundraiser. We should be putting people into office based on who has the best capabilities for the job and who has the best ideas. We could eliminate campaign contributions from corporations and unions, and prohibit money from out-of-state contributors in local elections. We could be the generation who takes the "For Sale" sign down next to the White House and the Capitol.

3. We could be the generation to create a high-performance government. How can you have a high-performance team when you can't fire the C and D players? It cannot be done. Why do we tolerate a poor-performing government when we the people own the government? Abolish government unions and give the power back to the people. It is a decision that will be in the best interests of the United States.

4. We could be the generation that fixes Social Security. An amazing program that has done so much for so many hangs by a thread because Congress won't deal with it. In one day, we could make sure that Social Security is a solid program that every American can count on for the future.

5. We could be the generation that makes President Eisenhower proud by curtailing the military–industrial complex. We spend more money on defense than the next seven nations combined. Much of it is warranted, yet much of it is not. The time has come to spend less on defense so that we can pay our bills.

6. We could be the generation that rebuilds America's infrastructure by raising the gas tax by $1, and we could be the generation that takes a global leadership role by reducing our greenhouse gas emissions. By raising the gas tax, we could take America's infrastructure, which is currently rated a D+, and make it the envy of the world. What Eisenhower did in the 1950s with building the interstate system, this generation could do for the 21st century. We have great ideas on how to get it done, and absolutely no political will to find the funds to build an infrastructure for future generations  that could make America more competitive, increase our quality of living, and put millions of Americans to work. This generation could be the one to rebuild America and to take a leadership role in global climate change.

7. We could be the generation to fix the tax code. Our generation has piled up a tax code of 74,608 pages. We could be the generation to put an end to the madness and have a 10-page tax return. It can be done!

8. We could be the generation to fix our legal system. We have four times the number of lawsuits per person than our friends in Canada, and we imprison more people than anyone in the world. We have more than 2.2 million people in prisons all across America—that translates to 750 per 100,000 people. In the 1970s, that number was 100. We could be the generation that put the people first and the lawyers second and create more legal reform in one year than the amount of reform created over the last 200 years.

9. We could be the generation to fix the health care system. We are the unhealthiest generation in the history of America. We could be the generation who looks at ourselves in the mirror and says, "The health of our people is poor, and our health care system is out of control. We are going to fix it." And with some bold decisions, this generation could significantly increase the health of our citizens and decrease the cost of the most expensive health care system in the world.

10. We could be the generation to rid the world of nuclear weapons. We should currently be scared stiff over the number of nuclear weapons that exist in the world and the ability of terrorist organizations to acquire nuclear weapons. It is time for America to take a global leadership role in reducing the chance for nuclear Armageddon. We can clean up our own house first and be an example to the rest of the world. Reduce our arsenal from 5,113 active missiles to 311. Pledge to the world that we will not use our nuclear forces as a first-strike option. We could be the generation to bring the nuclear age under control and take the first major step since the advent of the nuclear age to bring it to an end.

11. We could be the generation to reduce the issue of inequality in our country. Over the last 30 years, America's famous middle class has shrunk, and our citizens at the bottom of the ladder have less hope for the future. With a few bold moves, we could reduce childhood poverty by 50 percent and give every kid a chance to achieve the American dream.

12. We could be the generation to implement real gun control so that 12,000 Americans are not dying in our streets, and an additional 75,000 are not wounded. We can do all of this and still let proud gun owners use their guns to go hunting and to protect themselves at home. America is the most violent country in the world, and this is the generation that could change that.

"Don't waste a crisis."

One of my favorite quotes is "Don't waste a crisis." Well, we have a crisis in America. We have a dysfunctional government, more than 12,000 of our fellow citizens are gunned down in our streets yearly, we have a national debt over $19 trillion that needs to be repaid, we have a tax system that is 74,608 pages long, we have the most unhealthy generation in the history of America, we have a transportation system that is rated a D+, we have 5,113 nuclear missiles that are one accident away from blowing up the world, we have a campaign finance system that favors the rich and threatens our democracy, and we have done very little to reduce global warming. Sound horrible? It is.

Unfortunately, no one has really put all of these problems together and called this a true crisis. There is no real leadership in this country, no one willing to get in front of the group and lead. To let people know that we have real problems, and educate the American public on what the stakes are if we don't face the crisis that is upon us. We need some real leadership to sound the alarm, rally the American people, and offer some simple, bold solutions to save America. This can be done; we just need people to put the country first and their personal interests second, and by doing so, we can create an amazing future for the United States of America. ★

Epilogue

Thank you for taking the time to read this book. I have been asked by people who have read the book, "What can I do? How can I help change the direction of our country?" Here is my list:

1. Have an open mind. We have too much conflict in this country between Republicans and Democrats. Don't follow the party line. Think for yourself. Listen to others, especially those who have different views. Respect everyone and be open to what they have to say.

2. Write a note to your congressperson, senator, or state representative advocating for the ideas in this book that you agree with. A simple note letting *your* representative know what is on your mind can go a long way. Something as simple as:

   Dear Senator Brown,

   I hope you are well. I am concerned about the future of our country. I think as a nation we should look at making some big changes so that the next generation is in a better position than we are. The following are changes that I would like to see in our country. Since you are my representative, I am passing them along:

3. Write a note to the president of the United States. A short note goes a long way. Something like this:

Dear President Smith,

I know that you are a busy person so I will make this short. I think we have some big problems in our country, and I wanted to share some of my thoughts on specific changes that I think would make a big difference in the future of our country. Here is my list:

Address:
The White House
1600 Pennsylvania Avenue
Washington, D.C. 20500

4. Take responsibility for your health. The biggest problem that our nation will face from a financial standpoint in the next 20 years is the cost of health care. Call your doctor and sign up for a physical. Ask the doctor to give it to you straight. "How is my health?" "If you were me, what would you do?" Don't take responsibility just for your health, but make sure your kids are making healthy choices. The simplest way we can reduce the cost of health care in this country is to have healthy people.

5. Ask the CEO of your company to make the health of your fellow employees a high priority. There are many great examples of successful companies and organizations that have made a big difference.

6. Send a note to the NRA if you are a gun owner. Let the NRA know that you support gun rights, but you would like to see the following changes, and then list them.

7. Show compassion and help someone out who cannot help him- or herself. There are a lot of people in this country who need help. Volunteer some of your time, and give some of your money to those who need it the most.

Bottom line: JUST DO SOMETHING! ★

Endnotes

Dedication

Epigraph: Panel Four of Jefferson Memorial, Washington, D.C. Copy and original source available at: www.monticello.org/site/jefferson/quotations-jefferson-memorial#_note-9.

Introduction

[1]For national debt, see *U.S. Debt Clock.org*. Available at: www.usdebtclock.org/index.html (Accessed April 27, 2016). For pages of tax code, see Jason Russell, "Look at How Many Pages Are in the Federal Tax Code," *Washington Examiner,* April 15, 2015. Available at: www.washington examiner.com/look-at-how-many-pages-are-in-the-federal-tax-code/article/2563032. For the effects of global warming, see Union of Concerned Scientists, *Climate Change in the United States: The Prohibitive Costs of Inaction,* August 2009, p. 1. Available at: www.ucsusa.org/sites/default/files/legacy/assets/documents/global_warming/climate-costs-of-inaction.pdf. For Congress's approval rating, see "Congress and the Public," *Gallup,* no date. Available at: www.gallup.com/poll/1600/congress-public.aspx (accessed April 27, 2016).

Core Beliefs

[1] *U.S. Debt Clock.org*. Available at: www.usdebtclock.org/index.html. "(Accessed April 27, 2016)."

[2] Reported in Joel Klein, "The Failure of American Schools," *The Atlantic,* June 2011. Available at: www.theatlantic.com/magazine/archive/2011/06/the-failure-of-american-schools/308497/.

[3] Also reported in Klein, "The Failure of American Schools."

[4] "Child Poverty," *National Center for Children in Poverty* webpage, no date. Available at: www.nccp.org/topics/childpoverty.html (Accessed April 26, 2016).

[5] U.S. Energy Information Administration, "International Energy Data and Analysis," *EIA Beta* website, no date. Available at: www.eia.gov/beta/international/ (Accessed April 26, 2016). Click on "Consumption."

[6] American Society of Civil Engineers, "Bridges: Conditions & Capacity," 2013 Report Card for America's Infrastructure, March 2013. Available at: www.infrastructurereportcard.org/a/#p/bridges/conditions-and-capacity.

[7] Jonathan Weisman, "Senate Democrats Offer a Budget, Then the Amendments Fly," *The New York Times,* March 22, 2013. Available at: www.nytimes.com/2013/03/23/us/politics/senate-democrats-offer-a-budget-then-the-amendments-fly.html.

[8] Jason Russell, "Look at How Many Pages Are in the Federal Tax Code," *Washington Examiner,* April 15, 2015. Available at: www.washingtonexaminer.com/look-at-how-many-pages-are-in-the-federal-tax-code/article/2563032; Glenn Kessler, "How Many Pages of Regulations for 'Obamacare'?" *The Washington Post,* May 15, 2013. Available at: www.washingtonpost.com/blogs/fact-checker/post/how-many-pages-of-regulations-for-obamacare/2013/05/14/61eec914-bcf9-11e2-9b09-1638acc3942e_blog.html.

[9] "Over-Regulated America," *The Economist,* February 18, 2012. Available at: www.economist.com/node/21547789.

[10] U.S. Government Accountability Office, *2013 Annual Report: Actions Needed to Reduce Fragmentation, Overlap, and Duplication and Achieve Other Financial Benefits,* April 2013. Available at: www.gao.gov/assets/660/653604.pdf.

[11] Quoted in Walter Isaacson, "How Steve Jobs' Love of Simplicity Fueled a Design Revolution," *Smithosonian.com,* September 2012. Available at: www.smithsonianmag.com/arts-culture/how-steve-jobs-love-of-simplicity-fueled-a-design-revolution-23868877/?no-ist.

1. Fix Congress

[1] "Congress and the Public," Gallup, no date. Available at: www.gallup.com/poll/1600/congress-public.aspx (accessed April 27, 2016)

[2] Jonathan Weisman, "Senate Democrats Offer a Budget, Then the Amendments Fly," *The New York Times,* March 22, 2013. Available at: www.nytimes.com/2013/03/23/us/politics/senate-democrats-offer-a-budget-then-the-amendments-fly.html.

[3] Jon Terbush, "What It Costs to Win a Congressional Election," *The Week,* March 11, 2013. Available at: http://theweek.com/articles/466798/what-costs-win-congressional-election.

[4] Communications, "Money Wins Presidency and 9 of 10 Congressional Races in Priciest U.S. Election Ever," *OpenSecrets.org: Center for Responsive Politics,* November 5, 2008. Available at: www.opensecrets.org/news/2008/11/money-wins-white-house-and/.

⁵ Public Citizen Congress Watch, *Congressional Revolving Doors: The Journey from Congress to K Street,* July 2005, p. 6. Available at: www.lobbyinginfo.org/documents/RevolveDoor.pdf.

⁶ Dan Friedman, "Former Congressmen Make Huge Salaries as Lobbyists While Still Collecting Congressional Pensions," *New York Daily News,* May 24, 2014. Available at: www.nydailynews.com/news/politics/congressman-bank-lobbyists-article-1.1804659.

⁷ Mike Masnick, "Elected Officials Get an Average 1,452% Salary Increase When They Take a Lobbying Job," *Techdirt,* March 16, 2012. Available at: www.techdirt.com/articles/20120315/23155418121/elected-officials-get-average-1452-salary-increase-when-they-take-lobbying-job.shtml.

⁸ Ezra Klein, "14 Reasons Why This Is the Worst Congress Ever," *The Washington Post,* July 13, 2012. Original URL: www.washingtonpost.com/blogs/ezra-klein/wp/2012/07/13/13-reasons-why-this-is-the-worst-congress-ever/ (link no longer active). For information about the previous Congresses, including the numbers of bills passed, see www.senate.gov/pagelayout/reference/two_column_table/Resumes.htm.

⁹ "Wealth of Congress Index," *Roll Call,* last updated November 2, 2015. Available at: http://media.cq.com/50Richest/.

¹⁰ Katelin P. Isaacs, *Retirement Benefits for Members of Congress* (Congressional Research Service), July 31, 2015. The exact average given in the report is $41,652, and is for the 250 members who retired under the Federal Employment Retirement System (FERS) system in 2014. Available at: www.senate.gov/CRSReports/crs-publish.cfm?pid=%270E%2C*PLC8%22%40%20%20%0A.

¹¹ Paul Singer, "Office Budget Cuts Pose Challenges for Some House Members," *USA Today,* April 6, 2012. Available at: http://usatoday30.usatoday.com/news/washington/story/2012-04-02/congress-office-cutbacks/54055458/1.

¹² Gregory Smith, "R.I. Gov. Lincoln Chafee Says Governors in 46 States Have Line-Item Veto Authority," PolitiFact, October 6, 2013. Available at: www.politifact.com/rhode-island/statements/2013/oct/06/lincoln-chafee/ri-gov-lincoln-chafee-says-governors-46-states-hav/.

¹³ John Paul Stevens, *Six Amendments: How and Why We Should Change the Constitution* (New York: Little, Brown and Company, 2014): p. 33.

¹⁴ Stevens, *Six Amendments,* p. 39.

2. Reform Campaign Finance

[1] Communications, "Money Wins Presidency and 9 of 10 Congressional Races in Priciest U.S. Election Ever," *OpenSecrets.org: Center for Responsive Politics,* November 5, 2008. Available at: www.opensecrets.org/news/2008/11/money-wins-white-house-and/.

[2] Jon Terbush, "What It Costs to Win a Congressional Elections," *The Week,* March 11, 2013. Available at: http://theweek.com/articles/466798/what-costs-win-congressional-election.

[3] Quoted in Evan Osnos, "The Money Midterms: A Scandal in Slow Motion," *The New Yorker,* October 22, 2014. Available at: www.newyorker.com/news/daily-comment/money-midterms-scandal-slow-motion.

[4] Quoted in Clyde Haberman, "The Cost of Campaigns," *The New York Times,* October 19, 2014. Available at: www.nytimes.com/2014/10/20/us/the-cost-of-campaigns.html.

[5] Alexander Hamilton, James Madison, and John Jay, *The Federalist Papers,* edited by Clinton Rossiter, with an introduction and notes by Charles R. Kesler (New York: Signet Classics, 2003), pp. 323–24.

3. Create a High-Performance Government

[1] Quoted in Daniel Disalvo, "The Trouble with Public Sector Unions," *National Affairs* no. 5, Fall 2010. Available at: www.nationalaffairs.com/publications/detail/the-trouble-with-public-sector-unions.

[2] Dennis Cauchon, "Some Federal Workers More Likely to Die Than Lose Jobs," *USA Today,* July 19, 2011. Available at: http://usatoday30.usatoday.com/news/washington/2011-07-18-fderal-job-security_n.htm.

[3] Quoted in Angie Drobnic Holan, "Firing Federal Workers Is Difficult," *PolitiFact,* September 5, 2007. Available at: www.politifact.com/truth-o-meter/article/2007/sep/05/mcain-federal/.

[4] David Von Drehle, "Why Illinois Is Going Bankrupt," *Time,* January 18, 2013. Available at: http://swampland.time.com/2013/01/18/why-illinois-is-going-bankrupt/.

[5] Andrew G. Biggs, "Public Employee Pensions Must Be on the Table," *The New York Times,* December 5, 2013. Available at: www.nytimes.com/roomfordebate/2013/12/05/the-public-pension-problem/public-employee-pensions-must-be-on-the-table.

[6] Disalvo, "The Trouble with Public Sector Unions."

[7] Quoted in Disalvo, "The Trouble with Public Sector Unions."

[8] Andrew J. Coulson, "A Less Perfect Union: How the NEA and AFT Play Monopoly with Your Kids," *The American Spectator,* June 2011. Available at: http://spectator.org/articles/37510/less-perfect-union.

[9] Quoted in Jay P. Greene, "Steve Jobs on Education," *Education Next,* October 6, 2011. Available at: http://educationnext.org/steve-jobs-on-education/.

[10] Quoted in Gregg Keizer, "Jobs Bashes Teachers Unions," *PCWorld,* February 20, 2007. Available at: www.pcworld.com/article/129214/article.html.

4. Fix Social Security

[1] "Policy Basics: Top Ten Facts about Social Security," *Center on Budget and Policy Priorities,* August 13, 2015. Available at: www.cbpp.org/research/social-security/policy-basics-top-ten-facts-about-social-security.

[2] From excerpts of a speech by Frank Bane, "Problems of Social Security," *America's Town Meeting of the Air,* December 10, 1936. Available at: www.ssa.gov/history/banesp.html.

[3] "Child Poverty," *National Center for Children in Poverty* webpage, no date. Available at: www.nccp.org/topics/childpoverty.html.

[4] "Policy Basics: Top Ten Facts about Social Security."

[5] "Policy Basics: Top Ten Facts about Social Security."

[6] Paul Starr, "Why We Need Social Security," *The American Prospect,* February 2005. Available at: www.princeton.edu/~starr/articles/articles05/Starr-SocSec-2-05.htm.

[7] "Policy Basics: Top Ten Facts about Social Security."

[8] "Policy Basics: Top Ten Facts about Social Security."

[9] Steven Sass, Alicia H. Munnell, and Andrew Eschtruth, *The Social Security Fix-It Book* (Boston: Center for Retirement Research at Boston College, E-book Edition, 2009), p. 6.

[10] Martha M. Hamilton, "Washington Cannot Seem to Fix Social Security. Maybe You Should Try," *The Washington Post,* September 21, 2014. Available at: www.washingtonpost.com/news/get-there/wp/2014/09/21/washington-cannot-seem-to-fix-social-security-maybe-you-should-try/.

[11] Sass, Munnell, and Eschtruth, *The Social Security Fix-It Book,* p. 18.

[12] Steve Vernon, "The Real Reason Behind Social Security's Problems," *CBS Money Watch*, November 6, 2013. Available at: www.cbsnews.com/news/the-real-reason-behind-social-securitys-problems/.

[13] Figure determined based on supplied wage data and number of people (https://www.socialsecurity.gov/cgi-bin/netcomp.cgi?year=2014) and OASDI contribution rate (https://www.ssa.gov/OACT/ProgData/taxRates.html).

[14] Emily Brandon, "5 Ways to Fix Social Security," *U.S. News and World Report*, posted on *Huffington Post*, February 18, 2013. Available at: www.huffington-post.com/2013/02/18/change-social-security_n_2708000.html.

[15] David C. John, "Three Social Security Fixes to Solve the Real Fiscal Crisis," *The Heritage Foundation*, December 19, 2012. Available at: www.heritage.org/research/reports/2012/12/3-social-security-fixes-to-solve-the-real-fiscal-crisis.

[16] Reported in Steve Kroft (produced by James Jacoby and Michael Karzis), "Disability, USA," *60 Minutes*, aired on October 10, 2013. Script available at: www.cbsnews.com/news/disability-usa/.

[17] Reported in Steve Kroft, "Disability, USA."

[18] Reported in Steve Kroft, "Disability, USA."

[19] Reported in Steve Kroft, "Disability, USA."

[20] Steve Kroft, "Disability, USA."

5. Cut Defense Spending

[1] Quoted in Jon Basil Utley, "16 Ways to Cut Defense Spending," *The American Conservative*, February 22, 2013. Available at: www.theamericanconservative.com/articles/16-ways-to-cut-defense-spending-7/.

[2] Bob Burnett, "Why We Should Reduce the Defense Budget," *The Huffington Post*, April 19, 2013. Available at: www.huffingtonpost.com/bob-burnett/why-we-should-reduce-the-_b_3115515.html.

[3] "The U.S. Spends More on Defense Than the Next Seven Countries Combined," *The Peter G. Peterson Foundation*, April 12, 2015. Available at: www.pgpf.org/Chart-Archive/0053_defense-comparison.

[4] Jim Arkedis, "Time to End Supplemental Budgeting," *Progressive Policy Institute*, June 30, 2010. Available at: www.progressivepolicy.org/issues/budget/time-to-end-supplemental-budgeting/.

[5] Utley, "16 Ways to Cut Defense Spending."

[6] For military bases in the United States, see David Vine, "The Hidden Costs of Empire," *The American Conservative*, December 11, 2012. Available at: www.theamericanconservative.com/articles/the-hidden-costs-of-empire/. For military bases outside the United States, see David Vine, "The United States Probably Has More Foreign Military Bases Than Any Other People, Nation, or Empire in History," *The Nation*, September 14, 2015. Available at: www.thenation.com/article/the-united-states-probably-has-more-foreign-military-bases-than-any-other-people-nation-or-empire-in-history/.

[7] Much of the preceding section about weapons manufacturing comes from Utley, "16 Ways to Cut Defense Spending."

[8] As reported in Kate Brannen, "U.S. Army to Congress: No New Tanks, Please," *Defense News*, March 7, 2012. Available at: www.defensenews.com/article/20120307/DEFREG02/303070011/U-S-Army-Congress-No-New-Tanks-Please.

[9] Laura Litvan and Julie Bykowicz, "Defense-Cut Hypocrisy Makes GOP Converge with Democrats," *Bloomberg Business*, February 19, 2013. Available at: www.bloomberg.com/news/articles/2013-02-20/defense-cut-hypocrisy-makes-gop-converge-with-democrats.

[10] For the data on the F-35, and Senator McCain's quotes, see Kathleen Miller, Tony Capaccio, and Danielle Ivory, "Flawed F-35 Too Big to Kill as Lockheed Hooks 45 States," *Bloomberg Business*, February 22, 2013. Available at: www.bloomberg.com/news/articles/2013-02-22/flawed-f-35-fighter-too-big-to-kill-as-lockheed-hooks-45-states.

[11] Utley, "16 Ways to Cut Defense Spending."

[12] Arkedis, "Time to End Supplemental Budgeting."

[13] Unless indicated otherwise, the following list, including facts, figures, and quotes, is adapted from Melvin Goodman, "9 Ways to Reduce Defense Spending," *Huffington Post*, March 5, 2013. Available at: www.huffingtonpost.com/melvin-goodman/nine-ways-to-reduce-defen_b_2808002.html.

[14] Christian Davenport, "Why John McCain Called This $13 Billion Aircraft Carrier a 'Spectacular' Debacle," The Washington Post, October 1, 2015. Available at: www.washingtonpost.com/news/checkpoint/wp/2015/10/01/why-john-mccain-called-this-13-billion-aircraft-carrier-a-spectacular-debacle/.

[15] "The U.S. Spends More on Defense," *The Peter G. Peterson Foundation*.

[16] "Eligibility for Military Retirement Pay," Defense Finance and Accounting Service, page last updated March 31, 2015. Available at: www.dfas.mil/retiredmilitary/plan/eligibility.html. [16] Dwight D. Eisenhower, "The Farewell Address," delivered January 17, 1961. Available at *American Rhetoric: Top 100 Speeches,* www.americanrhetoric.com/speeches/dwightdeisenhowerfarewell.html.

[17] Dwight D. Eisenhower, "The Farewell Address," delivered January 17, 1961. Available at *American Rhetoric: Top 100 Speeches,* www.americanrhetoric.com/speeches/dwightdeisenhowerfarewell.html.

[18] Koba, "U.S. Military Spending Dwarfs the Rest of the World."

[19] Eric Boehm, "Defense Contractors Spend Millions Lobbying Congress, Get Billions in New Budget," *Watchdog.org,* January 22, 2014. Available at: http://watchdog.org/124909/defense-spending/.

6. Increase the Gas Tax and Save the World at the Same Time

[1] American Society of Civil Engineers, *2013 Report Card for America's Infrastructure,* March 2013. Available at: www.infrastructurereportcard.org/a/#p/home.

[2] The New York Times Editorial Board, "Highways Need a Higher Gas Tax," *The New York Times,* July 15, 2014. Available at: www.nytimes.com/2014/07/16/opinion/16wed1.html.

[3] The Rambler (Richard Weingroff), "Ask the Rambler: When Did the Federal Government Begin Collecting the Gas Tax?" *US Department of Transportation, Federal Highway Administration* website, November 18, 2015. Available at: www.fhwa.dot.gov/infrastructure/gastax.cfm.

[4] Cited in Union of Concerned Scientists, *Climate Change in the United States: The Prohibitive Costs of Inaction*, August 2009, p. 1 and p. 3. Available at: www.ucsusa.org/sites/default/files/legacy/assets/documents/global_warming/climate-costs-of-inaction.pdf.

[5] Cited in "Climate Change: What Do We Know?" *NASA: Global Climate Change: Vital Signs of the Planet* website, site last updated September 24, 2015. Available at: http://climate.nasa.gov/evidence/.

[6] Cited in Union of Concerned Scientists, *Climate Change in the United States*, p. 2.

[7] Quoted by Jordyn Phelps, "President Obama Says Global Warming Is Putting Our Safety in Jeopardy," *ABCNews.com*, September 22, 2009. Available at: http://blogs.abcnews.com/politicalpunch/2009/09/president-obama-says-global-warming-is-putting-our-safety-in-jeopardy-.html.

[8] Union of Concerned Scientists, "Ten Personal Solutions to Global Warming," *Union of Concerned Scientists* website, no date. Available at: www.ucsusa.org/global_warming/what_you_can_do/ten-personal-solutions-to.html#.VglQ2WBX_ww (Accessed April 26, 2016).

[9] "Scientific Consensus: Earth's Climate Is Warming," *NASA: Global Climate Change: Vital Signs of the Planet* website, site last updated September 24, 2015. Available at: http://climate.nasa.gov/scientific-consensus/. Webpage includes statements from 18 scientific associations that endorse the position that human activity is causing climate change.

[10] Keith Laing, "Dem Rep Moves to Increase Gas Tax by 15 Cents," The Hill, October 30, 2015. Available at: http://thehill.com/policy/transportation/258715-dem-rep-moves-to-increase-gas-tax-by-15-cents.

[11] George Voinovich, a retired senator from Ohio, appealed to Reagan's words to support an increase in the gas tax. See Kelly Phillips, "Former GM Exec Bob Lutz Suggests Higher Gas Taxes Would Help Americans," *Forbes,* April 27, 2013. Available at: www.forbes.com/sites/kellyphillipserb/2013/04/27/former-gm-exec-bob-lutz-suggests-higher-gas-taxes-would-help-americans/.

[12] "Carbon Tax or Cap-and-Trade?" *David Suzuki Foundation* website, no date. Available at: www.davidsuzuki.org/issues/climate-change/science/climate-solutions/carbon-tax-or-cap-and-trade/ (Accessed April 26, 2016).

[13] Alex Nussbaum, Mark Chediak, and Zain Shauk, "George Shultz Defies GOP in Embrace of Climate Adaptation," *Bloomberg,* November 30, 2014, updated December 1, 2014. Available at: www.bloomberg.com/news/articles/2014-12-01/reagan-statesman-s-sunshine-power-hint-of-thaw-in-climate-debate.

[14] American Society of Civil Engineers, "Transit," in *2013 Report Card for America's Infrastructure,* March 2013. Available at: www.infrastructurereportcard.org/a/#p/transit/overview.

7. Simplify the Tax Code

[1] The list is partly adapted from J. Juliet, "Benefits of Paying Taxes," *BenefitOf.net*, updated September 6, 2011. Available at: http://benefitof.net/benefits-of-paying-taxes/.

[2] Dean Reynolds, "Tax Code Too Complicated for Many Filers," *ABC News*, April 15 (no year provided). Available at: http://abcnews.go.com/WNT/story?id=129739&page=1.

[3] "Tax Reform in America: Simpler, Fairer, Possible," *The Economist*, July 13, 2013. Available at: www.economist.com/news/leaders/21581738-imperfect-proposal-could-still-improve-americas-awful-tax-code-back-it-mr-president-simpler.

[4] John McCormack, "GE Filed 57,000-Page Tax Return, Paid No Taxes on $14 Billion in Profits," *The Weekly Standard*, November 17, 2011. Available at: www.weeklystandard.com/blogs/ge-filed-57000-page-tax-return-paid-no-taxes-14-billion-profits_609137.html.

[5] Nina Olson, National Taxpayer Advocate, reported in Ellen Kant, "A Stark Reminder of the Excessive Cost of Complying with the Tax Code," *Tax Foundation*, January 15, 2013. Available at: http://taxfoundation.org/blog/stark-reminder-excessive-cost-complying-tax-code. For 104 changes to the NFL since 2001, see "NFL Rules History," *Steelerfury.com*, 2014. Available at: http://www.steelerfury.com/drupal/?q=node/3.

[6] Nina Olson, National Taxpayer Advocate, reported in Ellen Kant, "A Stark Reminder."

[7] For these and other loopholes, see Josh Dzieza, "8 Ridiculous Tax Loopholes: How Companies Are Avoiding the Tax Man," *The Daily Beast*, February 25, 2012. Available at: www.thedailybeast.com/articles/2012/02/25/8-ridiculous-tax-loopholes-how-companies-are-avoiding-the-tax-man.html.

[8] McCormack, "GE Filed 57,000-Page Tax Return."

[9] Jay MacDonald, "5 Taxes That Favor the Rich," *Bankrate.com*, no date. Available at: www.bankrate.com/finance/taxes/tax-deductions-favor-rich-1.aspx (Accessed April 26, 2016)

[10] Some of these solutions come from Erskine Bowles and Alan Simpson's Zero Plan for deficit reduction. See "The Bowles-Simpson 'Chairmen's Mark' Deficit Reduction Plan," *Tax Policy Center*, no date. Available at: www.taxpolicycenter.org/taxtopics/Bowles_Simpson_Brief.cfm (Accessed April 26, 2016).

¹¹ Cass R. Sunstein, "How to Simplify the Tax Code. Simply," *Time*, May 31, 2013. Available at: http://ideas.time.com/2013/05/31/how-to-simplify-the-tax-code-simply/.

¹² Jeanne Sahadi, "Bowles and Simpson Detail $2.5 Trillion Deficit Reduction Plan," *CNN Money*, April 18, 2013. Available at: http://money.cnn.com/2013/04/18/news/economy/bowles-simpson-deficits/.

8. Fix the Legal System

¹ Quoted in Jeff Jacoby, "US Legal Bubble Can't Pop Soon Enough," *Boston Globe*, May 9, 2014. Available at: www.bostonglobe.com/opinion/2014/05/09/the-lawyer-bubble-pops-not-moment-too-soon/qAYzQ823qpfi4GQl2OiPZM/story.html.

² Jacoby, "US Legal Bubble Can't Pop Soon Enough,".

³ "Guilty as Charged," *The Economist*, February 2, 2013. Available at: www.economist.com/news/leaders/21571141-cheaper-legal-education-and-more-liberal-rules-would-benefit-americas-lawyersand-their.

⁴ Dorothy Gambrell, "The 113th Congress, by the Numbers," *Bloomberg Business*, January 10, 2013. Available at: www.bloomberg.com/bw/articles/2013-01-10/the-113th-congress-by-the-numbers.

⁵ Adam Liptak, "U.S. Prison Population Dwarfs That of Other Nations," *The New York Times*, April 23, 2008. Available at: www.nytimes.com/2008/04/23/world/americas/23iht-23prison.12253738.html?pagewanted=all.

⁶ Liptak, "U.S. Prison Population."

⁷ Liptak, "U.S. Prison Population."

⁸ Justices Rehnquist and Kennedy are quoted in Eve Tushnet, "Fifteen to Life: 15 Ways to Fix the Criminal Justice System," *Crisis Magazine*, March 1, 2003. Available at: www.crisismagazine.com/2003/fifteen-to-life-15-ways-to-fix-the-criminal-justice-system.

9. Fix the Health Care System

[1] Bloomberg Best (and Worst), "Most Efficient Health Care 2014: Countries," *Bloomberg,* August 25, 2014. Available at: www.bloomberg.com/visual-data/best-and-worst/most-efficient-health-care-2014-countries.

[2] Barack Obama, "Remarks by the President at the Opening of the White House Forum on Health Reform," *The White House, Office of the Press Secretary,* March 5, 2009. Available at: www.whitehouse.gov/the-press-office/remarks-president-opening-white-house-forum-health-reform.

[3] Quoted in Chris Strauss, "Gary Player Blasts America's 'Tsunami of Obesity'," *For the Win,* July 9, 2013. Available at: http://ftw.usatoday.com/2013/07/gary-player-blasts-americas-obesity-problem. From USA Today—(Academic Permission), July 9, 2013 © 2013 Gannett-USAToday. All rights reserved. Used by permission and protected by the Copyright Laws of the United States. The printing, copying, redistribution, or retransmission of this Content without express written permission is prohibited.

[4] Steven Brill, "Bitter Pill: Why Medical Bills Are Killing Us," *Time,* April 4, 2013. Available at: http://time.com/198/bitter-pill-why-medical-bills-are-killing-us/.

[5] Social Security Advisory Board, *The Unsustainable Costs of Health Care,* September 2009, p. 1. Available at: http://ssab.gov/portals/0/documents/TheUnsustainableCostofHealthCare_508.pdf.

[6] "The Facts on Medicare Spending and Financing," *The Henry J. Kaiser Family Foundations,* July 24, 2015. Available at: http://kff.org/medicare/fact-sheet/medicare-spending-and-financing-fact-sheet/.

[7] *The Long-Term Budget Outlook and Options for Slowing the Growth of Health Care Costs: Testimony Before the Comm. of Finance,* 110th Cong. (2008) (statement of Peter R. Orszag, Director of the Congressional Budget Office): p. 1. Available at: www.cbo.gov/sites/default/files/110th-congress-2007-2008/reports/06-17-ltbo_testimony.pdf.

[8] Atul Gawande, "The Cost Conundrum: What a Texas Town Can Teach Us about Health Care," *The New Yorker,* June 1, 2009. Available at: www.newyorker.com/magazine/2009/06/01/the-cost-conundrum.

[9] Brill, "Bitter Pill."

[10] Brill, "Bitter Pill."

[11] George S. McGovern, "The Simple Health-Care Solution: Medicare for Everyone," *The Washington Post,* September 13, 2009. Available at: www.washingtonpost.com/wp-dyn/content/article/2009/09/11/AR2009091102406.html.

[12] Brill, "Bitter Pill."

[13] Brill, "Bitter Pill."

[14] The 30 years are 1980–2010. Reported in Christopher Ingraham, "The Average American Woman Now Weighs as Much as the Average 1960s Man," *The Washington Post,* June 12, 2015. Available at: www.washingtonpost.com/news/wonk/wp/2015/06/12/look-at-how-much-weight-weve-gained-since-the-1960s/.

[15] Dan Witters, "U.S. Obesity Rate Climbs to Record High in 2015," *Gallup,* February 12, 2016. Available at: www.gallup.com/poll/189182/obesity-rate-climbs-record-high-2015.aspx?g_source=CATEGORY_WELLBEING&g_medium=topic&g_campaign=tiles.

[16] Centers for Medicare & Medicaid Services, "On Its 50th Anniversary, More than 55 million Americans Covered by Medicare," *CMS.gov,* July 28, 2015. Available at: www.cms.gov/Newsroom/MediaReleaseDatabase/Press-releases/2015-Press-releases-items/2015-07-28.html.

[17] Bloomberg Best (and Worst), "Most Efficient Health Care 2014."

[18] Rick Blizzard, "Healthcare Systems Ratings: U.S., Great Britain, Canada," *Gallop,* March 25, 2003. Available at: www.gallup.com/poll/8056/Healthcare-System-Ratings-US-Great-Britain-Canada.aspx?g_source=canada%20health%20care&g_medium=search&g_campaign=tiles.

[19] McGovern, "The Simple Health-Care Solution."

[20] Centers for Disease Control and Prevention, "Cigarette Smoking Among Adults—United States, 2006," *Morbidity and Mortality Weekly Report,* November 9, 2007. Available at: www.cdc.gov/mmwr/preview/mmwrhtml/mm5644a2.htm.

10. Reduce the Risk of Nuclear War

[1] Ashley Lutz, "This Chart Shows the Terrifying Power of Modern Nuclear Bombs," *Business Insider,* June 19, 2012. Available at: www.businessinsider.com/this-chart-shows-the-terrifying-power-of-modern-nuclear-bombs-2012-6.

[2] Steven Starr, "Cold War Has Thawed Only Slightly," *Nuclear Darkness, Global Climate Change & Nuclear Famine: The Deadly Consequences of Nuclear War* website, no date. Available at: www.nucleardarkness.org/solutions/disarmamentversusdeterrence/.

[3] Quoted and cited in Walter Isaacson, *Einstein: His Life and Universe* (New York: Simon & Shuster, 2007): p. 494. Original source is an interview with Alfred Werner, in *Liberal Judaism*, April–May 1945.

[4] Ed Pilkington, "US Nearly Detonated Atomic Bomb over North Carolina—Secret Document," *The Guardian,* September 20, 2013. Available at: www.theguardian.com/world/2013/sep/20/usaf-atomic-bomb-north-carolina-1961.

[5] Special Guest Star, "8 Nuclear Weapons the U.S. Has Lost," *Mental Floss,* November 29, 2007. Available at: http://mentalfloss.com/article/17483/8-nuclear-weapons-us-has-lost.

[6] Michael Dobbs, "The Real Story of the 'Football' That Follows the President Everywhere," *Smithsonian.com,* October 2014. Available at: www.smithsonianmag.com/history/real-story-football-follows-president-everywhere-180952779/?no-ist.

[7] Hiram Maxim and Orville Wright quoted in Martin E. Hellman, "On the Probability of Nuclear War," a 1985 op-ed now found on author's university website, under "Opinions." Website: http://ee.stanford.edu/~hellman/. Article available at: www-ee.stanford.edu/~hellman/opinion/inevitability.html.

[8] Martin E. Hellman, "How Risky Is Nuclear Optimism?" *Bulletin of the Atomic Scientists* 67, no. 2 (2011): p. 49. Available at: www-ee.stanford.edu/~hellman/publications/75.pdf.

[9] "Nuclear Weapons: Who Has What at a Glance," *Arms Control Association,* June 23, 2014. Available at: www.armscontrol.org/factsheets/Nuclearweaponswhohaswhat.

[10] "50 Facts about U.S. Nuclear Weapons Today," *Brookings Institute,* April 28, 2014. Available at: www.brookings.edu/research/articles/2014/04/28-50-nuclear-facts.

[11] Quoted in Martin E. Hellman, "Nuclear War: Inevitable or Preventable?" in *Breakthrough: Emerging New Thinking* (New York: Walker and Co., 1988), pp. 80–85. Online version of chapter available at: www-ee.stanford.edu/~hellman/Breakthrough/book/chapters/hellman.html.

[12] "Nuclear Weapons: Who Has What at a Glance," *Arms Control Association.*

[13] "Nuclear Weapons: Who Has What at a Glance," *Arms Control Association.*

[14] Hellman, "Nuclear War: Inevitable or Preventable?"

[15] Hellman, "How Risky Is Nuclear Optimism?" p. 49.

[16] "50 Facts about U.S. Nuclear Weapons Today," *Brookings.*

[17] Quoted in Michael Crowley, "Yes, Obama Really Is Worried about a Manhattan Nuke," *Time,* March 26, 2014. Available at: http://time.com/39131/barack-obama-nuke-manhattan-new-york/.

[18] Dan Farber, "Nuclear Attack a Ticking Time Bomb, Experts Warn," *CBS News,* May 4, 2010. Available at: www.cbsnews.com/news/nuclear-attack-a-ticking-time-bomb-experts-warn/.

[19] Quoted in Martin E. Hellman, "How Risky Is Nuclear Optimism?" p. 50. For the documentary *Nuclear Tipping Point,* see www.nucleartippingpoint.org/home.html.

[20] Gary Schaub Jr. and James Forsyth Jr., "An Arsenal We Can All Live With," *The New York Times,* May 23, 2010. Available at: www.nytimes.com/2010/05/24/opinion/24schaub.html?_r=0.

[21] Alan Phillips and Steven Starr, "Change Launch on Warning Policy," *Nuclear Darkness, Global Climate Change & Nuclear Famine: The Deadly Consequences of Nuclear War* website, no date. Available at: www.nucleardarkness.org/solutions/changelaunchonwarning/.

[22] "Eliminate High-Alert, Launch-Ready Nuclear Weapons," *Nuclear Darkness, Global Climate Change & Nuclear Famine: The Deadly Consequences of Nuclear War* website, no date. Available at: www.nucleardarkness.org/solutions/eliminatehighalertnuclearweapons/.

[23] Matthew Bunn, *Securing the Bomb 2010: Securing All Nuclear Materials in Four Years,* April 2010, p. 69. Available at: www.nti.org/media/pdfs/Securing_The_Bomb_2010.pdf?_=1317159794.

[24] An excerpt of the speech can be found at "A Roadmap for Peace," *Nuclear Darkness, Global Climate Change & Nuclear Famine: The Deadly Consequences of Nuclear War* website, no date. Available at: www.nucleardarkness.org/solutions/mccloyzorinaccords/.

11. Reduce Inequality in America

[1] Shiller quoted in John Christoffersen, "Rising Inequality 'Most Important Problem,' Says Nobel-Winning Economist," *St. Louis Post-Dispatch*, October 14, 2013. Available at: www.stltoday.com/business/local/rising-inequality-most-important-problem-says-nobel-winning-economist/article_a5065957-05c3-5ac0-ba5b-dab91c22973a.html;

[2] Congressional Budget Office, *Trends in the Distribution of Household Income between 1979 and 2007,* October 2011, p. ix. Available at: www.cbo.gov/sites/default/files/112th-congress-2011-2012/reports/10-25-HouseholdIncome_0.pdf.

[3] John Cassidy, "American Inequality in Six Charts," *The New Yorker,* November 18, 2013. Available at: www.newyorker.com/news/john-cassidy/american-inequality-in-six-charts.

[4] Hope Yen, "U.S. Poverty: Census Finds Nearly Half of Americans Are Poor or Low-Income," *Huffington Post,* December 17, 2011. Available at: www.huffingtonpost.com/2011/12/15/census-shows-1-in-2-peopl_1_n_1150128.html.

[5] Reported in Charles M. Blow, "Reducing Our Obscene Level of Child Poverty," *The New York Times,* January 28, 2015. Available at: www.nytimes.com/2015/01/28/opinion/charles-blow-reducing-our-obscene-level-of-child-poverty.html. For the OECD's rankings of countries by relative child poverty rates, Blow is citing Children Defense Fund, *Ending Child Poverty Now,* 2015. Available at: www.childrensdefense.org/library/PovertyReport/EndingChildPovertyNow.html.

[6] Blow, "Reducing Our Obscene Level of Child Poverty."

12. Reduce Gun Deaths in America

[1] "Gun Violence by the Numbers," Everytown For Gun Safety Fund, no date. Available at: https://everytownresearch.org/gun-violence-by-the-numbers/#America (accessed April 27, 2016).

[2] Data are yearly averages from 2010–2014. See "Gun Death and Injury 5 Year Average Stat Sheet," *Brady Campaign*, December 18, 2015. Available at: www.bradycampaign.org/sites/default/files/Gun%20Deaths%20Fact%20Sheet_Mar2016.pdf. See also: www.bradycampaign.org/key-gun-violence-statistics.

3 Simon Rogers, "Gun Homicides and Gun Ownership listed by Country," *The Guardian*, July 22, 2012. Available at: www.theguardian.com/news/datablog/2012/jul/22/gun-homicides-ownership-world-list#data.

4 "Jennifer Norberry, Derek Woolner, Kirsty Magarey, "After Port Arthur—Issues of Gun Control in Australia," Current Issues Brief 16 (1995–96). From Parliament of Australia Library. Available at: www.aph.gov.au/About_Parliament/Parliamentary_Departments/Parliamentary_Library/Publications_Archive/CIB/cib9596/96cib16.

5 Mark Follman, Julia Lurie, Jaeah Lee, and James West (based on research by Ted Miller, "What Does Gun Violence Really Cost?" *Mother Jones*, May/June 2015. Available at: www.motherjones.com/politics/2015/04/true-cost-of-gun-violence-in-america.

6 Mark Follman, Gavin Aronsen, Deanna Pan, and Maggie Caldwell, "US Mass Shootings, 1982-2015: Data from Mother Jones' Investigation," *Mother Jones,* December 28, 2012, last updated July 16, 2015. Available at: www.mother-jones.com/politics/2012/12/mass-shootings-mother-jones-full-data.

7 Christopher Ingraham, "Shooting in Oregon: So Far in 2015, We've Had 274 Days and 294 Mass Shootings," *Washington Post*, October 1, 2015. Available at: https://www.washingtonpost.com/news/wonk/wp/2015/10/01/2015-274-days-294-mass-shootings-hundreds-dead/.

8 Ezra Klein, "Twelve Facts about Guns and Mass Shootings in the United States," *The Washington Post,* December 14, 2012. Available at: www.washingtonpost.com/news/wonkblog/wp/2012/12/14/nine-facts-about-guns-and-mass-shootings-in-the-united-states/.

9 Quinnipiac University National Poll, "Iraq - Getting In Was Wrong; Getting Out Was Right, U.S. Voters Tell Quinnipiac University National Poll; 92 Percent Back Background Checks for All Gun Buys," July 3, 2014. Available at: www.quinnipiac.edu/news-and-events/quinnipiac-university-poll/national/release-detail?ReleaseID=2057. PolitiFact's PunditFact cites numerous polls that have reached similar percentages. See Lauren Carroll, "Laura Ingraham Wrongly Says Claim That 90% Support for Gun Background Checks Has Been Debunked," PunditFact, January 5, 2016. Available at: www.politifact.com/punditfact/statements/2016/jan/05/laura-ingraham/laura-ingraham-say-claim-90-support-gun-background/.

10 Quoted in John Paul Stevens, *Six Amendments: How and Why We Should Change the Constitution* (New York: Little, Brown and Company, 2014): p. 127.

[11] Suggested revision of Second Amendment is John Paul Stevens's. See Stevens, *Six Amendments*, p. 132.

[12] Mark Follman and Gavin Aronsen, " 'A Killing Machine': Half of All Mass Shooters Used High-Capacity Magazines," *Mother Jones,* January 30, 2013. Available at: www.motherjones.com/politics/2013/01/high-capacity-magazines-mass-shootings.

[13] Fareed Zakaria, "The Solution to Gun Violence Is Clear," *The Washington Post,* December 19, 2012. Available at: www.washingtonpost.com/opinions/fareed-zakaria-the-solution-to-gun-violence-is-clear/2012/12/19/110a6f82-4a15-11e2-b6f0-e851e741d196_story.html.

[14] Brady Campaign to Prevent Gun Violence, "Key Gun Violence Statistics."

[15] Joel Benenson and Katie Connolly, "Don't Know Much about Gun Laws," *The New York Times Sunday Review,* April 6, 2013. Available at: www.nytimes.com/2013/04/07/opinion/sunday/dont-know-much-about-gun-laws.html?_r=0.

• • •

Acknowledgments

Thank you to everyone who contributed to this book. I have a selective memory, not by choice. The good news is that I have a very good memory about the things that my mind cares about. I wrote this book after I heard David McCullough challenge the Marquette graduating class to "[And] sometime at some point do something for your country." I will forever remember that. I want to thank everyone who touched this book and turned an idea into reality.

I have had some great helpers along the way. I want to thank my old college roommate Mark Murphy, who went through the manuscript many times and provided valuable feedback. I want to thank my long-time friend and co-worker Pat Sullivan, who read the manuscript numerous times and had amazing feedback on a couple of key issues. I want to thank Carl Stratman for editing the book. Carl was timely, to the point, and did an awesome job. Many thanks to Kristin Mitchell from Little Creek Press. Kristin provided great feedback and brought the book to life with an excellent layout. I want to thank David Hackworthy Jr., who helped out at the start of the project. I want to thank a number of friends who read the manuscript and gave great advice. Thank you Chad Brown, Bob Burns, Mark Joslyn, Dr. Mark Timmerman, and Dave Reinecke. I also want to thank my mother, who helped out with the design of the cover. My CEO (Chief Empathy Officer) is my assistant Cindy Wagner. I have been lucky enough to work with Cindy for over 20 years and she helped out on the project. A big thank you goes to my wife Tania, who did whatever was asked when it came to the book. ★

About the Author

John Burke began working at Trek Bicycle in 1984 and has been president of the company since 1997. In addition to leading Trek, John served as chairman of President George W. Bush's President's Council on Physical Fitness and Sports and is a founding member of the Bikes Belong Coalition. John is an avid cyclist who has finished Ironman Wisconsin twice as well as completing the Boston and New York Marathons. John and his wife, Tania, live in Madison, Wisconsin. ★